Quilting Curves

An Innovative Technique

for Machine-Piecing Curves

with Incredible Ease

Vikki Pignatelli

THE QUILT DIGEST PRESS

NTC/Contemporary Publishing Group

Library of Congress Cataloging-in-Publication Data

Pignatelli, Vikki.
    Quilting curves : an innovative technique for machine-piecing curves with incredible ease / Vikki
Pignatelli.
        p.   cm.
    ISBN 0-8442-4249-7
      1. Appliqué—Patterns.   2. Quilts.   I. Title.
TT779.P493   2001
746.46—dc21   00-56129

*I dedicate this book to the Holy Spirit who has generously blessed me with
inspiration, discovery, creativity, and the opportunity to share these gifts with others.*

Editorial and production direction by Anne Knudsen
Art direction by Kim Bartko
Project editing by Julia Anderson
Interior design by Hespenheide Design
Interior photography by Sharon Hoogstraten
Drawings and photos on pages 39 and 88–89 by Vikki Pignatelli
Manufacturing direction by Pat Martin

Published by The Quilt Digest Press
A division of NTC/Contemporary Publishing Group, Inc.
4255 West Touhy Avenue, Lincolnwood (Chicago), Illinois 60712-1975 U.S.A.
Printed and bound in Singapore by Star Standard Industries, Ltd.
International Standard Book Number: 0-8442-4249-7
01 02 03 04 05 06 SS 18 17 16 15 14 13 12 11 10 9 8 7 6 5 4 3 2 1

CONTENTS

Life Beyond, 2000, 62″ × 86″ (157 cm × 218 cm).

Even though winter is associated with the death of living things, there is life beyond what we are able to see.
At Blacklick Pond, the inspiration for this quilt, everything seems to have died. But look closely and you will
see goldfish swimming beneath the ice.

A New Way of Quilting

For as long as I can remember, the curved shape has always appealed to me, whether in nature or art. So it's no surprise that when I began quilting, I was enticed by quilts with beautiful curved patterns that swept gracefully across the surface. At quilt shows and in magazines, I was immediately drawn to quilts that featured intricate curves or waves of bold color. I marveled at the gracefulness and beauty of such designs and tried to figure out how they were made. My imagination was teeming with all sorts of ideas for designs I wanted to try. I had a clear picture of the effect I wanted to create in my quilts, but I had no inkling of how to begin.

Books I read and classes I attended helped me learn about quiltmaking, but none showed me how to create in fabric the images that were so clear in my mind's eye. I learned about curved piecing, which is done either by easing seams together or by using a reverse appliqué technique, with satin stitch. Neither curved piecing nor using satin stitch was suitable for me. I could not get my seams to lie flat using conventional piecing techniques. Nor was I happy with the overall effect satin stitch gave my quilts. I was frustrated to the point of tears. I finally decided I was on my own and needed to work out for myself a method that would capture the grace and motion I wanted in my quilts. It also had to be easy—I was not an experienced sewer.

After much trial and error, a technique I dubbed mosaic appliqué was born. This topstitch technique is a fast and simple way to achieve the grace and beauty of curves in a quilt top without the painstaking precision that conventional piecing entails. The result is a quilt top that appears to be intricately pieced. How is it possible to construct such difficult curves with such incredible ease? The answer is a technique that combines surface piecing and appliqué layering using freezer-paper templates and fabric stabilizer. Each piece is sewn in a predetermined numerical order onto a stabilizer foundation. The templates are *machine-blindstitched* to each other *on the surface* of the quilt top. There is no need for the precise seam measurements that conventional piecing requires, nor for the

Breaking Point

The story of my own discovery of quilt-making is one of personal joy and sadness. Over the years, I have tried out many crafts, yet my first love was oil painting. With only books and a few art classes at a local craft store to learn from, I taught myself to paint landscapes and family portraits. Then in 1981, my mother became ill with cancer. With her death came the death of the creativity I'd known. To this day, I've never picked up another paintbrush.

I dabbled in other crafts, including hand-sculpted dolls, until my sister persuaded me to attend a quiltmaking class with her. I was reluctant at first, but to my surprise, I ended up loving it! As I would discover, I'd found a new way to paint, this time with fabric instead of brushes.

In the midst of my excitement, my husband, like my mother, was diagnosed with cancer. Our family had a couple of rough years, with stresses and crises at every turn, until I felt that I was reaching the breaking point. I used my quiltmaking to keep my mind occupied, yet I fully expected my newfound love would fade, as had my love of oil painting when my mother became ill. Then one afternoon I watched as a storm battered and bent a tree in our front yard, expecting the tree to snap under the onslaught. The tree, too, was at the breaking point, but with remarkable flexibility it was able to weather the storm.

Like the tree, I found new strength to cope with life's troubles and set out to design a quilt that would help me remember that moment of discovery. I wanted my quilt to depict the tree twisting in the wind against a stormy sky. I envisioned a quilt full of curves in constant motion, capturing the violence I'd witnessed and the movement of the wind-battered tree. Yet when I tried to create those tortuous curves in fabric, conventional quiltmaking techniques didn't work. When I put the very first two templates together, I just couldn't get the seams to lie flat. I knew there had to be an easier way. Through trial and error, persistence, and sheer determination, I finally figured it out. Within a year, I had honed the technique to the method described in this book.

Happily, my husband's cancer was curable, and today he is a cancer survivor. The quilt I made is a reminder of those tough times we faced together. While I was still working on *Breaking Point*, a second storm roared through and this time snapped the entire middle trunk off the tree that had been my inspiration. A third storm later in the year broke off another huge branch. A neighbor offered to cut down the tree for us, but I didn't have the heart to destroy it. I patched its wounds with tar and hoped it would live. The tree still stands today, scarred by the storms that are a fact of its life, yet—just as my family was able to overcome sorrows—it continues to grow and thrive.

tricky needle turns or seam allowances associated with appliqué. Patterns come together quickly and easily, with beautiful, graceful results. Even if you are a beginning quilter, as I was, you will be able to make a perfectly pieced quilt top.

One of the delights of topstitch piecing is that since you are working on the surface of the quilt top through the entire project, the design is always visible to you as it progresses. This means the technique allows not just for greater accuracy but for an incredible amount of versatility. Since you can see exactly what and where you are sewing at all times, it is easy to achieve perfect matches with every seam. You simply make any adjustments you need right on top of the stabilizer before you sew. Also, it is possible to change or modify your original design as you go along, altering colors and lines as your quilt top begins to take on a life of its own. It is even easy to single out a particular object in a fabric pattern —such as a pretty butterfly or leaf—and position it exactly where you want it on the quilt.

As I continued to experiment, I discovered that the topstitch piecing method has limitless applications. It is not just a method for constructing curves.

Breaking Point, 1995, 48" × 40" (122 cm × 100 cm).
I made Breaking Point *during a period of high stress. The tree represents the individual and the wind and rain are the inevitable storms of life we must all endure. One way to survive is to bend and ride out the storm instead of fighting against it. I was inspired to make this quilt as I watched a beautiful tree in our yard buffeted by a spring storm.*

It is just as easy to use to create geometric patterns and straight lines. Another appealing benefit, particularly for those who have difficulty with precision piecing, is that this technique is excellent for incorporating long, narrow points, such as star points. Folk art, pictorials, crazy quilts, and especially landscapes are best suited to the technique, but it can even work with some traditional quilting blocks as well.

In *Quilting Curves*, you will first learn the basics of this new and exciting quilting method by making a simple quilt top. You will then be able to choose from seven more quilt top patterns, each using the technique for different effects. You will learn manipulation techniques to enhance your quilt top with dimension and texture. You can achieve a unique look in your quilts when you use curved borders and apply bindings that are an extension of the quilt pattern. You can practice new stitching motifs and learn how to use multiple threads and a single needle to express your creativity with free-motion stitching. Best of all, you will see how simple it is to take this method and strike out on your own, creating curved quilt patterns with ease and confidence.

Nikki Pignatelli

Blacklick Pond: Reflections at Twilight, 1995, 53" × 55" (135 cm × 137.5 cm).

Blacklick Woods is a beautiful metropolitan park near our home. I often retreat into the woods to enjoy and draw upon the peace and solitude that enhances creativity. Within the park is a quiet and secluded pond that is the inspiration for this quilt. It represents summertime—a busy, vibrant season teeming with life. In summer the pond flourishes with raucous, gleeful song and lush colors.

Before You Begin

As the old cliché goes, "If all else fails, read the directions." We're all guilty of skipping over the preliminaries at one time or another in anticipation of starting a new project. You will find that some of the methods I use—both for creating the quilt top and adding the quilting—are new to you. Before you begin, I want to stress the importance of making the right preparations and having the right tools and supplies at hand. Take time to read through this section carefully—you'll find you refer back to it often as you work.

Tools and Supplies

Always choose the best tools and materials you can find or afford. It doesn't make sense to put in precious time and energy and end up with a quilt that is less than perfect. Many quilters I know blame themselves if their piecing or quilting is less than perfect. All too often, the problem is that the tools they use are not up to the task. You deserve better! Topstitch piecing requires no special tools that you have not employed for other quiltmaking methods. The one exception is the flexible curve, an inexpensive tool used to draw curves. Before you begin, make sure you have the following items ready to use. All are available at your local quilt and fabric shops or at art supply stores.

Sewing Machine

A quality sewing machine is your best friend. Service it on a regular basis to keep it in tip-top shape and it will reward you many times over. Oil and clean your machine regularly, according to the manufacturer's directions for your make and model. Renegade threads and lint can build in and around the bobbin and affect the quality of the stitching. I use a soft watercolor paintbrush to clear away debris from these areas.

Walking foot

Open appliqué foot

Open darning foot

A standard sewing machine, with a few special features or decorative stitches, is fine for topstitch piecing. Most of the projects in this book use the blindstitch, which is standard on newer models. You will need the following machine feet:

- Walking foot: ensures an even feed of all fabric layers through the machine while stitching.
- Open appliqué foot: enables you to see clearly what and where you are stitching. Optimum visibility is crucial, too, for good results.
- Open darning foot: provides good visibility for free-motion quilting.

Stabilizer

No-stretch fabric stabilizer is the key to the topstitch piecing technique. All the templates are sewn directly onto a foundation stabilizer, which remains in place throughout construction. Even after the quilt top is completed, the stabilizer is not removed, but becomes part of the quilt.

Stabilizer keeps the uncut freezer-paper templates correctly positioned and the prepared fabric templates in place during the stitching process. It also keeps seams from puckering. By using stabilizer, you are able to arrange and pin several fabric pieces together before sewing. This way, you can really see the quilt top take shape and make any necessary color or measurement adjustments before you stitch the pieces in place. Using a stabilizer foundation keeps the pieced quilt top from stretching out of shape. It also adds the necessary density and stability you'll need while machine or free-motion quilting, eliminating the need for a hoop.

Also, I have found that using stabilizer when working with printed patterns or motifs in fabric allows me more freedom. I can arrange templates exactly as I please, without having to consider whether the pattern falls on the lengthwise or crosswise grain of the fabric. If a fabric has a butterfly motif, for instance, I can arrange the template to include the butterfly in the exact position I want. It doesn't matter that the template is cut on the bias, since the stabilizer prevents it from stretching once it is stitched down.

There are two commercially available stabilizers that I use in my quilts. One is Pellon stabilizer by Freudenberg Nonwovens, and the other is Pattern-Ease by Handler Textile Corporation. Both products are nonwoven and have no stretch. Pellon comes in several weights and measures 22″ (55 cm) in width. I recommend the lightweight density (#30 weight) for your quilting projects. For a larger quilt, you need to bond the edges of two or more sheets together with a roll of ¾″ (2 cm) fusible web. Pattern-Ease comes 46″ (112 cm) wide and is a bit more convenient for big projects.

Do not use tear-away or iron-on stabilizers. Besides being more expensive, tear-away stabilizers are meant to be removed. For this technique, you want the stabilizer to remain in place after construction to avoid stretch in your quilt top and to stabilize your machine quilting. Iron-on stabilizers are not suitable because they expose and accentuate hidden seam allowances beneath the surface after they're fused and are difficult to remove if you decide to change a fabric template.

Threads

Since all stitching is completed on the surface and is visible, you will need fine-quality threads in a variety of colors that match, blend with, or contrast with the fabrics in your quilt. If you are comfortable using an invisible thread, that is certainly an option for you. I use polyester threads for surface sewing and a regular-weight, medium-color gray thread for the bobbin. You may include embroidery rayon, twisted metallic and ribbon metallic threads (such as Sulky Sliver®), and other favorite specialty threads for the finishing touches. Use these threads for quilting, decorative surface stitching for crazy quilts, or thread painting—enhancing or accenting an area in the quilt top, such as a leaf, with layers of stitches.

Needles

For piecing, use universal sewing machine needle size 80/12. For free-motion or machine quilting, I recommend a size 90/14 topstitch needle. I use mostly metallic and rayon threads in my quilts and find this needle, which has a bigger eye and longer shank, gives me the best results and fewer thread breakage problems, even with multiple threads/single needle use.

Curves

The flexible curve is an invaluable and fun tool for designing curves. It is an implement made of a rubberlike material with wire inside. It varies in length from 18″ or 24″ up to 36″ (45 cm or 60 cm up to 90 cm). It is very narrow, about ½″ (1.5 cm) in width, and maneuvers easily to form snaking curves. Twist or bend it to the shape you want and use it as an aid to tracing the shape or curve onto drawing paper.

Another tool to consider is a French curve set. This is a set of curves made from clear, rigid plastic, which comes in graduated sizes. The curves on these sets are smaller and tighter than the curves you can get with the flexible curve.

The flexible curve and French curve set are available from quilt shops, office supply stores, and art supply stores.

Light Table

Use a professional light table or improvise by placing a small lamp underneath a glass dining or coffee table and turning off the overhead lights. Alternatively, tape the project to a window and work by daylight.

Battings

There are many fine commercial battings on the market today. Select the batting that has the correct properties for the project you are making. These are some questions to ask yourself: Is the project for use or for a wall hanging? Is warmth a factor for the quilt? Do I want a high-loft (fluffy), low-loft (flat), or antique appearance? How will the project be quilted? By hand or machine? How closely will it be quilted? Will it be laundered often? For the projects in this book, I recommend an 80 percent cotton/20 percent polyester batting with very low loft.

Other Essentials

Drawing paper

Freezer paper (for making templates), available from grocery stores

Waxed paper (for piecing bindings)

Sharp drawing pencils, #2 or #4 lead, and pencil sharpener

Quilt marking pencil

Eraser, a quality white plastic or vinyl eraser that will erase softly and completely
    without leaving marks

Drafting tape, ¾″ (2 cm) width (used for joining sheets of freezer paper or drawing paper when designing and for marking binding lines on a quilt)

Iron, in good condition, with a clean soleplate and a steam setting

Paper scissors

Fabric scissors, sharp and of high quality, used only for cutting fabric

Straight pins, sharp, stainless steel

Thread snips for clipping threads and seam ripper

Clear quilting rulers and square (for borders, corners, and squaring up
    the finished project)

Rotary cutter and mat

Metal yardstick and metal tape measure (as an aid for squaring up large quilts)

Fusible web (I use Stitch Witchery by Dritz, available in three weights: ultra light,
    regular, and super)

6″ (15 cm) extra long tweezers, with bent tips (for stuffing corners in templates)

Choosing Fabrics

Before I took up quilting, I painted in watercolor and oil. When I began working with fabrics, I was amazed to discover that the quiltmaker's palette is just as colorful as the painter's. When I look at fabric, I see an endless array of colors and patterns spread before me. They inspire images as diverse as bubbling water, misty rain, blowing wind, and glowing fire. Fabrics are rich with unique and glorious dashes of colors, minute details, textures, and patterns. It would be impossible to re-create this colorful riot of lines and details on canvas with a paintbrush. It is fabric that gives quiltmakers an advantage over painters. We have the freedom to use fabrics, with their endless nuances of color and texture, to "paint" our quilts, giving them free-flowing movement and dimension. I find that blending many different fabrics into a quilt is fun and a challenge to the imagination.

Types of Fabrics

Although almost any fabric can be used for topstitch piecing, I urge you to begin with 100 percent cotton fabrics. Cotton holds seam allowance creases well and is generally easy to manipulate. Expensive or fragile materials may fray easily or require special handling. It is better to concentrate on learning the technique than spend time fighting with fussy fabric.

Once you are familiar with the topstitch piecing technique, you may try velvet, satin, and lamé. Easy-fray materials such as lamé and satin should be stabilized on the wrong side using fusible iron-on interfacing. Stabilizing not only prevents fraying but gives substance to the fabric for easier handling.

For my quilts, I prefer to work with commercial batiks and multicolored hand-dyed fabrics rather than with solids or commercial prints with repeat patterns. Every inch of hand-dyed material is unique in color and design, and the templates made with it can be positioned, angled, and cut in countless ways. This presents artistic opportunities with color, lines, design, and movement.

Collecting Fabrics

Most quilters I've met own boxes of scraps and remnants they have been hoarding for years. Topstitch piecing can be a godsend for using favorite odds and ends. Since the quilts are not repeat designs or block patterns requiring certain amounts of identical fabrics, you may use bits and pieces of whatever you have in your stash. Many of the templates in the patterns in this book are small enough to be cut out from pieces of scrap material.

My own potpourri style of quilting evolved from my love of all colors and material. As an avid fabric junkie and collector, I have more fabric than I can use up in two lifetimes. I find it impossible to choose just a few fabrics to work with in a quilt. I love them all and use as many as I can—sometimes hundreds—in each quilt.

Buying Fabrics

I will use every conceivable excuse to buy material, but I seldom purchase it in large amounts. Nor will I buy all the fabric I need for a new quilt at one time. Instead, I buy only fabrics I love and can't live without and ones that "speak to me." I find most times these fabrics tend to work out better in my quilts than those purchased specifically for a quilt.

When looking for fabrics at a quilt shop, always stand away from the bolts before deciding on colors. If the colors run together, indistinguishable from a distance, this will also happen in your quilt. Always view your choices from a distance of at least 10 feet (3 meters). Remember, too, that shop lighting can change the overall appearance of a fabric color. If possible, view the fabric by a window or outdoors.

Reviewing Fabric Choices

Once you have made fabric selections for a quilt, set the fabrics up on a design wall in your sewing area. Stand back and view your choices to see how well they work together and to make sure there is enough contrast among them. Look for

Color Terms

The *value* of a color is its lightness or darkness on a scale from white to black. The color on the light end of the scale (white) is a high value. The color on the black end of the scale is the low value.

The *intensity* or *saturation* is the vividness or purity of a color. The purer the color, the higher the intensity. The more a color is diluted with white, gray, or black, the lower the intensity.

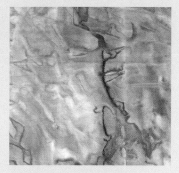

Value contrast (light/dark).

Color contrast (pink/green/purple/gold) and value contrast (light/dark).

Intensity contrast (pure pink/gray-pink), color contrast (red/green), and value contrast (light/dark).

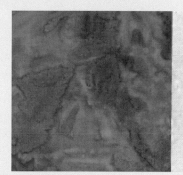

The bright green and blue are pure colors. Adding black, gray, or white lessens their intensity.

good contrasts in colors, value, and intensity. Rearrange them and add to them until you are satisfied with the color values. Make sure, too, that your selection represents a good range in pattern, line, shape, and size of the printed design. For more help in fabric selection, see "Choosing Colors" in Chapter 6.

Preparing Fabrics

Once you have made your fabric selections, I recommend that you prewash each piece. This way, you will know for sure that the materials will not shrink or bleed after you have put your heart, soul, and hard work into a quilt.

I do not use soap or detergent, but I do thoroughly rinse out all the fabrics I use. I usually just throw light fabrics, which are unlikely to bleed, in the cold-water rinse cycle of the washing machine and then let them tumble dry in the dryer. Fabrics with intense or dark colors, like some batiks and hand-dyed fabrics, do have a tendency to bleed. Test each piece before use. I hand-rinse those fabrics in the sink one at a time to see which ones have a problem with bleeding.

Batiks and Hand-Dyed Fabrics

One reason I love batiks and hand-dyed fabrics is that using them gives a distinct look to my work. Batiks often contain two or more colors that blend from one hue to another within the fabric. I call these *transitional fabrics*. I can achieve free-flowing movement easily in my work by using a variety of transitional fabrics to change from one color to the next across the background of the quilt.

For example, I may want to change the background color of my quilt from green to purple. By using a transitional fabric containing both green and purple, I can cut the fabric in such a way that the green in the transitional fabric will butt up to the green already in the background.

Because the transitional fabric contains some purple, too, the next fabric I choose will contain mostly purple. By butting up the purple in the transitional fabric with purple in the new fabric, I've created a smooth flow of color for the eye to follow. In addition, using transitional fabrics to meld colors gives my quilt the painted look I like in my work.

Besides color, many batiks and hand-dyed fabrics have lines and design patterns in them, produced when the material was folded or twisted during the dyeing process. If you carefully position the fabric when preparing the templates, the continuity of those lines and shapes can add to the sense of motion in the quilt.

Detail of Creation of the Sun and Stars. *See full quilt on page 84.*

Use transitional batiks that have a variety of colors in them to move from color to color and from light to dark. This example shows how I changed the background color in Creation of the Sun and Stars *(see page 84).*

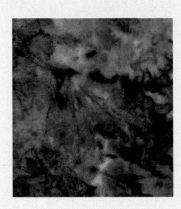 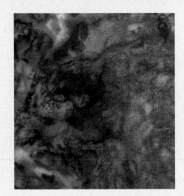 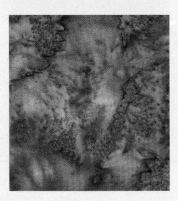

My preference for treating hand-dyed fabrics that bleed is to use a commercial chemical solution such as Synthrapol, distributed by G & K Craft Industries Limited. Synthrapol is used in a hot-water bath to remove the excess dye from hand-dyed fabrics. The hotter the water temperature, the better. This product does a wonderful job and is available in some quilt shops, at quilt shows, and by mail order. Always follow the manufacturer's directions when working with chemicals and, as a precaution, wear rubber gloves and make sure you have adequate ventilation.

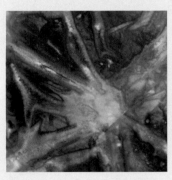

Another way to achieve movement is with lines, motifs, or dye-pattern shapes that are part of the fabric design. As shown in this detail of Creation of the Sun and Stars, *using a batik with divergent lines gives a newborn star the illusion of motion.*

Detail of Creation of the Sun and Stars. *See full quilt on page 84.*

Or, through the use of a shape created as a result of the dye process in hand-dyed fabric, the same quilt shows an explosion within a stream of flames.

Detail of Creation of the Sun and Stars. *See full quilt on page 84.*

Tears on Blacklick Pond, 1996, 60¾″ × 58″ (154 cm × 147 cm).
The colorful floating autumn leaves are beautiful at secluded Blacklick Pond, a metropolitan park near our home. I delight in these leaves falling around me, swirling in the breeze. Fall is my favorite time of year, yet it is bittersweet. The leaves are "tears," and their falling signals death, as associated with the season.

CHAPTER I

What Is Topstitch Piecing?

*T*opstitch piecing appliqué is a fast and simple technique that allows you to incorporate twisting curves and sharp points into your quilt tops without the difficulties associated with precision piecing or appliqué. It allows for perfect accuracy and an incredible freedom of design. The technique combines surface piecing with appliqué layering using freezer-paper templates and foundation stabilizer. Rather than coming together block by block, the quilt top builds gradually. It is easy to change colors or switch directions as you progress, since you are working entirely on the surface of the quilt top and can see the complete picture take shape. Like a landscape artist painting stroke after stroke onto canvas, you have the freedom to add fabric to fabric and color to color.

Spring Tulip, 1998, 16¾" × 14 (42 cm × 35 cm)

In this chapter, I will walk you through one of the first topstitch piecing quilt tops I made, explaining the technique and demonstrating its wonderful versatility. By following along with me as we make *Spring Tulip*, you will learn all of the fundamentals for making a topstitch piecing quilt top and will be ready to choose your next project from the patterns that follow in Chapter 2, "Seven Easy Patterns."

Making a Spring Tulip *Quilt Top*

This quilt top is fun and easy to make, even for the most inexperienced sewer. Choose 100 percent cotton for all fabrics. Choose colors for your tulip and leaves that are vivid, bright, and have good contrast between light and dark. If you are unsure, look at them from a distance of at least 10 feet (3 meters). For the background, you might choose a fabric with a pattern that simulates rain, wind, or has a moody feel to it. Avoid patterns that are too busy; they may overpower the tulip design. The border fabric should complement the background.

DIMENSIONS
16¾" × 14" (42 cm × 35 cm) with border
Note that tulip *only* is 9½" × 12" (23.75 cm × 30 cm)

MATERIALS
Tulip petals: scraps in three values of one color
Leaves: green scraps in four or five values
Background: ½ yd (50 cm) dark or grayed fabric
Stabilizer: 20" × 20" (50 cm × 50 cm) lightweight (30–35 wt)

Template Markings and What They Mean

The templates are probably like no others you have seen in quiltmaking, with far more numbers, marks, and arrows to trace. The markings may seem intimidating at first, but once you get used to them you will see how easy they are to use and you will appreciate how much they simplify the topstitch piecing technique.

- Numbers—indicate the order of cutting and sewing.
- Short arrows—indicate which side or sides of a template include a seam allowance that needs to be turned under to hide raw edges. Usually on

template 1 there is no need to turn under any seam allowances, since all raw edges are covered by subsequent templates.

- XX—means turn under the seam allowance to the line indicated, leaving remaining seam allowance flat.
- Hash marks—help you match up a prepared freezer-paper template to its correct position once it has been cut out from the rest of the uncut pattern.
- Long arrows—indicate directional flow of fabric (see page 8). Long arrows are helpful when using printed fabric with lines or curves to create the same sense of movement in your quilt.

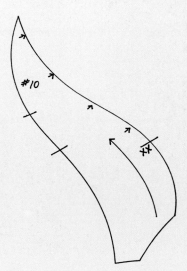

Markings on the templates indicate sewing order, seams to be turned under, and directional flow.

1. Photocopy the *Spring Tulip* pattern on pages 112–115, enlarging it if desired. Place the copy face up on a table and lightly tape down the corners to keep it from moving. Place a large sheet of freezer paper waxed side down on top of the design, completely covering it. Tape the freezer paper down also to avoid shifting. In most cases, the lines of the pattern are clearly visible through the freezer paper. If you have difficulty tracing the pattern through the freezer paper, work on a light table, a glass table, or a window to improve visibility.

2. Trace all lines on all twenty-four tulip templates onto the freezer paper, including the line marking the inner border. (Do not trace the outside border, templates 25 to 28, yet; the border and binding are not added until the tulip design is completed and sewn.) Also trace the short arrows that indicate which seams are to be turned over and the template numbers that indicate sewing order. If you are working with fabrics that have a directional pattern, trace the long arrows. These indicate the direction in which the template should "flow" (see page 8).

3. Cut your stabilizer at least 1″ (2.5 cm) larger on all sides than the desired size of your finished quilt. Remove the traced freezer-paper pattern from the table and pin it on top of the stabilizer foundation with quilter's pins. Pin it securely to avoid slippage. Do not cut away the excess stabilizer.

4. With sharp paper scissors, carefully cut out template 1 on the seam line, leaving the rest of the freezer-paper pattern intact and pinned to the foundation. Make sure you cut the freezer paper only and do not cut through to the stabilizer foundation. Do not cut out any other templates at this time.

5. Place template 1 waxed side down on the right side of the selected fabric. If the fabric has a directional pattern, use the long arrows to help you position the template on the material so you can get the correct flow. Using a steam iron on a cotton setting, iron the freezer paper onto the fabric. Press well, allowing no loose edges or points.

6. Adding a seam allowance of about ⅝″ (1.8 cm), cut the fabric around the template with sharp scissors. Increase the seam allowance to about ¾″ (2 cm) along the side of the template that overlaps the border. This compensates for any mistakes in construction and shrinkage during quilting and will ensure a well-fitted border. With topstitch piecing, it is fine to eyeball the seam allowance—there is no need to measure accurately. Remember, though, that there must be a seam allowance on every side of every paper template.

7. Return the freezer-paper/fabric template 1 to its place on the stabilizer foundation. Place it right side up in the hole you cut it out of, matching all the paper edges. By nudging the seam allowances beneath the surrounding freezer paper pattern, it should fit in place like the last piece of a jigsaw puzzle. Note that there is no need to turn under any seam allowances for this first piece, since all will be covered by subsequent pieces.

8. Beginning with the border edge, pin each side of the fabric template securely in place through the seam allowances only using small-head straight pins. Pin the fabric only, not the paper. Remove the freezer paper, loosening it by carefully running a straight pin or needle between the fabric and the paper and lifting the paper off gently. It should peel off easily. Pin the center of the template securely to the stabilizer.

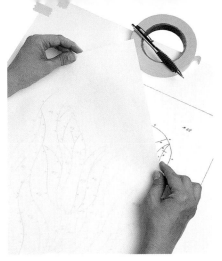

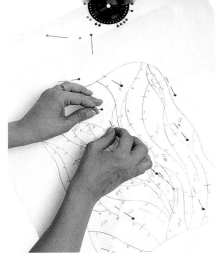

Step 1. Tape freezer paper shiny side down onto the design.

Step 2. Trace the pattern onto the freezer paper, complete with all arrows and numbers.

Step 3. Securely pin the traced freezer paper pattern to the stabilizer foundation.

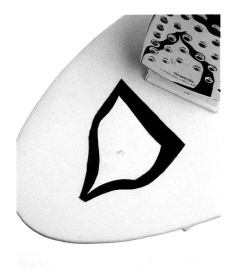

Step 4. Cut template 1 on the seam line, leaving the rest of the pattern intact. Do not cut through the stabilizer.

Step 6. Leave seam allowances on all sides, especially those that butt against a borderline.

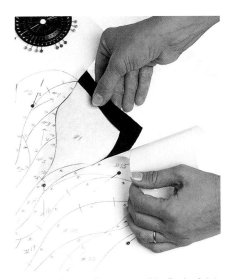

Step 7. Using cut lines as a guide, fit the fabric template back into the pattern as you would a jigsaw puzzle piece.

Step 8. Carefully remove the freezer paper once the fabric template is securely pinned in place.

Step 9a. Press the seam allowance underneath, using the paper edge as a guide.

Step 9b. Return the finished template to its place in the pattern. Template 2's turned-under seam allowance covers the raw edges of template 1.

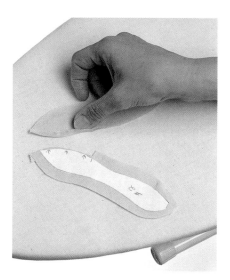

Step 10a. Clip the seam allowance of inward curves so they will lie flat.

Step 10b. Outward curves turn under more easily when you trim the seam allowance.

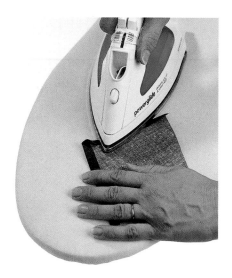

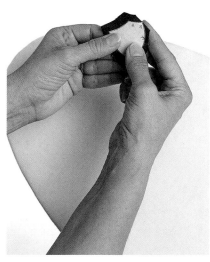

Step 10c. Finish corners by first turning under one side, and then the other.

Step 10d. To form angles that are not too acute, turn under the tip first and then one side.

Step 10e. Turn under the second side and tack it with fusible web.

9. Repeat Steps 4 through 8, cutting out template 2. For the edge that has small arrows, reduce the seam allowance to about ⅜″ (1 cm). Turn the edge under, using the edge of the freezer paper as a guide, and press. Strive for a smooth line along the template edge. Note that when it's repositioned on the foundation stabilizer, this finished edge will cover one of the raw edges on fabric template 1. When securing the fabric template, pin it right at the crease of the turned-seam allowance, attaching fabric template 2 to fabric template 1 and the foundation stabilizer. Avoid pinning through the freezer paper. Once the template is securely pinned in place, remove the freezer paper.

10. Continue cutting and repositioning the freezer-paper templates and replacing them on the foundation stabilizer with the fabric templates in numerical order until you have three to five of them in place. As a general rule, the smaller the pieces and the fewer the curves, the more you can handle as a single batch. Make sure the pieces fit smoothly in place. Keep the following guidelines in mind as you work.

- If the template edge to be turned under has concave, or inward, curve, you will need to clip the fabric seam allowance so that it lies flat. Clip the seam allowance almost to the freezer paper but not quite. Gentle curves need only a few shallow cuts, but moderate to sharp curves require more. There is no need to trim the seam allowance. Inward curves are simple and turn under beautifully, even with large seam allowances.
- If your template has convex, or outward, curves, take care in pressing them under. Ease them under slowly and gently so you can attain a smooth curve. Avoid jagged points. Sharp outward curves will turn under a little more easily if the seam allowance around the curve is trimmed to about ¼″ (0.75 cm). Do not trim the seam allowance too much! If you do get a point, use a dab of water on your finger to moisten that point and iron over it. Do not clip outward curves. It is unnecessary and creates points in the turned edge of the seam allowance, giving a jagged look to the template.
- To turn under seam allowance around curves, work with small amounts at a time. Press down each small length before progressing to the next until you've turned under the entire side.
- If the fabric has a tendency to fray, stabilize it with iron-on stabilizer before cutting and clipping, especially with fussy or fragile fabrics such as lamé.
- To reinforce deep clips made for tight curves and seal fabric to prevent fraying, apply pieces of fusible web, like Stitch Witchery, at the crease end of the cut to tack the turned seam allowance in place.
- To turn a corner, first turn under the seam allowance and press one side completely, and then turn under and press the other.
- To form points with angles that are not too acute, trim the seam allowance to ¼″ (0.75 cm). First, fold under the allowance across the very

- Make sure the iron's soleplate and vents are clean to avoid unwanted residue.
- Use a steam iron on a cotton setting. Seam allowance edges maintain a sharp crease longer with steam.
- If the freezer paper sticks stubbornly to the fabric and shreds when it is removed, the setting is too hot. In some cases, freezer paper will stick to gilded fabrics or those with metallic threads running through them. Lower the setting for these materials.
- Even if the paper does shred on a fabric template, it can be salvaged. Dampen the freezer-paper residue with a dab of water on a rag, a moistened finger, or water mist. Wait a moment, then scrape off the paper with your fingernail or a straight pin. Repeat if necessary.
- If the freezer paper refuses to adhere properly to a fabric, the iron is not hot enough or the fabric is damp. Raise the temperature slightly.
- With synthetic fabrics, lamé, wool, and other blends, use a steam iron on a lower setting. Also, it may be necessary to use a press cloth to protect sensitive fabrics. Test for the correct setting on a spare swatch of fabric before ironing the freezer paper to it.

Achieving Directional Flow in *Spring Tulip*

Note that several of the templates include long arrows, indicating directional flow (see my sketch of the leaf photo). The leaves are a good example. If the fabric you choose, like the green in my quilt, has a directional pattern, position the template so the long arrow corresponds to the fabric pattern. The leaf will "flow" in the same way. If a single leaf has two or more templates, you will see that each template indicates a different directional flow. The result is that the leaf appears to be twisting or bending.

Once you become confident with fabric selections and the topstitch piecing technique, add your own arrows indicating directional flow. Perhaps you would like your *Spring Tulip* to appear moody and include rain in the background. Choose a direction for the falling rain and mark each of the background templates with a long arrow accordingly.

When you first look at fabrics, consider which part of the design will make for the best movement in your quilt. I usually ignore fabric grain entirely in favor of zeroing in on the perfect area of the design that moves me or enriches my quilt. With the exception of oversized templates, you shouldn't encounter any bias stretch problems with topstitch piecing since the foundation stabilizer holds everything in place.

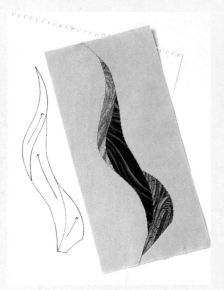

Use of directional flow enhances the illusion that the leaf is twisting.

Directional flow, indicated by arrows, simulates wind.

Here, directional flow simulates rain.

tip of the freezer-paper template corner toward the back. Press. Tack down the corner with fusible web to secure it, if desired. Next, turn under one side of the corner to the back, using the freezer-paper edges as a guide. Press it and tack it down. Turn the remaining side under. Press it, trim it if necessary, and tack it down.

• If you change your mind about fabric selections while preparing a fabric template, you may reuse the freezer-paper template several times before it loses its ability to stick to the fabric.

• Leave the remaining uncut freezer-paper design intact and pinned to the stabilizer foundation while you sew. It shouldn't get in the way, but

Some fabrics have printed patterns that flow; others simulate moving elements like wind or rain.

if you have difficulty, try rolling up the excess portion jelly-roll fashion so that it fits better under the sewing machine arm.

11. Begin sewing down the first batch of three to five templates. Work in numerical order again, referring back to the original pattern if necessary. Use the machine blindstitch (----^----^----^) set at a very short length. (For most machines the correct stitch length is 1.0 and the width is 2.0.) The stitch length between the jags (^) should be about ⅜″ (1 cm). Adjust the presser foot so it will run as close as possible along the edge of the fabric template. The tiny stitches (----) should remain on the bottom piece and the blindstitch (^) should catch the edge of the turned-over seam allowance.

Follow these guidelines as you sew:

• You may begin the stitching in a corner where two templates meet by taking a single stitch forward, reversing, and then stitching forward again to lock the stitches in place. End the stitching in the same way, with a locking stitch. Alternatively, if another template overlays the one you are sewing down, lift it a little so that you can start the stitching beneath it. You'll need to remove a straight pin or two to accommodate the sewing machine presser foot. Remember to replace the pins after you stitch.

• Neatly clip the thread tails at the surface.

• When sewing down curved templates, stitch slowly and raise the presser foot often (with the needle down) to accommodate the direction of the curve. Avoid the temptation to cheat by attempting to slide the fabric through the curve. It can distort the fabric and cause unwanted stretch in your quilt.

• Check to make sure that each template lies flat and smooth before you stitch it down.

• Do not be tempted to sew same-color templates at the same time to avoid changing threads. This can cause problems, especially when working with curves cut on the bias. For ease and neatness, keep to numerical order. That way, if a fabric template does stretch during stitching, you can smooth it and any excess material will be covered up by the next template. If you sew out of order and the succeeding template is already sewn down, the distortion is locked in place.

• Always sew from inside to outside; that is, begin sewing at the center and proceed toward the nearest border. Stitch away from previously

Step 11a. Use the machine-blindstitch for stitches that won't be noticeable when the quilt is finished.

Step 11b. The ^ jag of the stitch must catch the crease of the fabric template being sewn down.

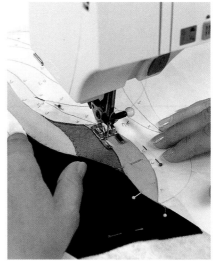

Step 11c. Sew down seams in an outward direction, away from other seams.

sewn seams, not toward them. This way, excess fabric will be hidden by the seam of a succeeding template.

　　　• Change needles often during sewing, especially if you hit a straight pin. Needle burrs snag and damage the fabric.

　　　• Not necessary but certainly handy are the "needle down" and "mirror image" stitching features available on newer sewing machines.

　12. After each set of three to five fabric templates is sewn in place, press well. When all templates are sewn, press again.

　　　Well done! In twelve easy steps, you have just completed your first top-stitch piecing project. Did you ever think quilting with curves would be this easy? You should be very proud and pleased with your efforts. You have learned the basics of a new technique that you can apply to many great sewing projects in the future.

Additional Techniques

Now that you understand and have practiced how topstitch piecing works, read through the rest of this chapter to learn additional techniques that will make your sewing easier, more accurate, and, of course, more attractive. You will then be ready to move on to other projects in the book, as well as thinking of other ways in which you can use the topstitch piecing method.

Lining a Template

When you construct any quilt, you use a combination of light and dark colors. Because of this, *shadowing*, the seam allowance of a dark fabric showing up beneath a light fabric on the surface, is unavoidable. In *Spring Tulip*, for example, if you use a light pastel for the flower petals or leaves, you will have a problem with shadowing. A simple solution is to line each of your light surface fabrics before sewing it down. This is how it is done.

　1. Place the freezer-paper template of the piece to be lined on a piece of densely woven white fabric or muslin and press. Cut the muslin template out, leaving small seam allowances on all sides of the template *except* the side or sides to be turned under (indicated by small arrows on the template). Cut that side or those sides directly on the seam line, without cutting the edge of the paper. Do not turn any seams under on this lining. Carefully remove the freezer paper and set the lining aside.

　2. Place the same freezer-paper template onto the light-colored fabric and press. Cut out the light-colored fabric template as usual, with applicable seam allowances and turned-under edges.

　3. Turn the light-colored template over to the wrong side. Turn over the muslin piece and align it on the wrong side of the light-colored template so that it fits the shape of the template identically.

Shadowing of Dark Fabrics

Sometimes, a dark-colored seam allowance from a preceding fabric template may show through the light color of an overlapping fabric template. This is called *shadowing*. Template 2, for example, is a tulip petal. If you've chosen a pastel for your flower, a darker fabric of template 1 is likely to show through. For an easy solution to masking dark fabrics, see "Lining a Template."

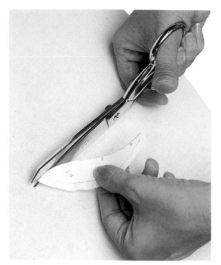

Step 1. Cut out the muslin lining, leaving a seam allowance on all sides except the edge to be turned under (indicated by small arrows).

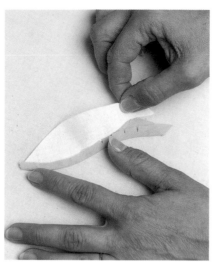

Step 3a. Flip over the muslin lining and fit it to the back of light-colored template.

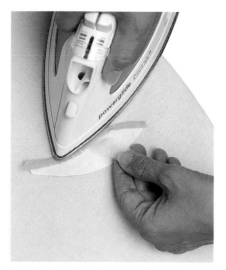

Step 3b. Tack down the seam allowance covering the muslin lining with fusible web.

The turned-under seam or seams of the light-colored template should overlap the white muslin. It is not necessary, but if you wish you can tack the turned-under seam or seams of the light-colored template to the lining with tiny pieces of fusible web to hold it in place until you sew it down.

4. Return the lined light-colored template to its place in the design, pin it down, and proceed with the next template.

Decorative Surface Stitches

I've suggested that for piecing templates you use the ----^----^----^ machine blind-stitch (or reversed, called the *shell stitch*). With this stitch, the only thread visible on the surface of the quilt is the ^ part of the stitch. When you use a matching or blending thread, the stitching becomes virtually invisible.

However, there may be times you wish to call attention to the stitching or accentuate it. You are free to use any contrasting color of thread for the stitches, or any type of decorative threads, such as rayons or metallics. If your machine is capable of making decorative stitches, you may use them to sew down the templates.

For each decorative stitch you choose, use the sewing foot recommended by the manufacturer. Center the decorative stitch over the seam line so that it hits both the top and bottom templates.

For the sake of neatness, you may want to begin the stitching underneath the seam of the succeeding template or plan your stitches so one stitch does not cover up or interfere with another. Utilizing various decorative stitches results in a crazy-quilt look and is an easy way to make beautiful quilts, gifts, and fun projects for the home.

Center the decorative stitch so that it hits both top and bottom templates.

Ripping Seams

As you sew, so shall you rip. To rip out machine blindstitching easily, turn the project over to see the ----^----^----^ bobbin thread on the stabilizer. With a sharp seam ripper, cut both slanted threads (^) of the jag the entire length of the seam to be ripped. Flip the project over right side up and lift the top thread from the surface. Brush off the leftover bobbin thread from the underside.

An alternative method is to rip the stitches from the surface of the project. Bend back the fabric templates to expose the stitches of the seam to be ripped out. Slide the lower tip of the seam ripper in between the top and bottom layers and slice through the stitches connecting those templates. While faster, this method is a little risky, as it requires good eyesight and a steady hand.

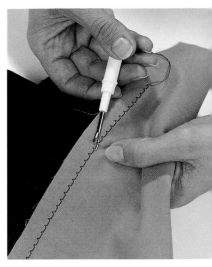

Cut both threads of the bobbin's ^ jag stitch for easy ripping.

In Review

The twelve easy steps to making a topstitch pieced quilt top are as follows:

1. Copy the pattern, enlarging it as necessary, and trace it onto the waxy side of a sheet of freezer paper.
2. Trace all numbers, marks, and arrows of the templates.
3. Cut a piece of stabilizer large enough to accommodate the freezer-paper pattern. Attach the freezer-paper pattern shiny side down to the stabilizer with straight pins.
4. Cut out the first freezer-paper template.
5. Iron the template shiny side down to the right side of the fabric.
6. Cut out the first fabric template, leaving the appropriate seam allowances on all sides.
7. Return the prepared fabric template to its place or hole in the design, using the edges of the freezer paper as a guide.
8. Pin down the fabric template through the seam allowances. Carefully remove the freezer paper and pin through the center of the fabric template.
9. Cut out the second freezer-paper template from the pattern, ironing it onto the right side of the fabric. Cut out the fabric template with seam allowances. Turn under the seam allowance or allowances as indicated by the small arrows and press. Pin fabric template into place in the design, using freezer-paper edges as a guide. Remove freezer paper.
10. Continue preparing the first batch of three to five templates.
11. Stitch the fabric templates onto the surface of the project, using the machine blindstitch to sew the turned-under seam allowance edge of the top template to the template beneath it.
12. Press the stitched-down templates. Continue piecing, stitching, and pressing templates in numerical order until all are finished.

Fire and Ice, 1995, 44" × 45" (112 cm × 114 cm), cotton.
This quilt is a study in colors and shapes. The flaming vivid red, yellow, and orange of fire is in direct contrast to the jagged icy blue, gray, and lavender of winter. The inspiration for this quilt was a comforting fire in our fireplace during a very cold winter's night!

CHAPTER 2

Seven Easy Patterns

The seven quilt top patterns in this chapter are all made using the same technique as *Spring Tulip* in Chapter 1. All are constructed on stabilizer foundation and machine-blindstitched. For many patterns I've provided some guidelines for choosing colors for your fabrics. There are patterns at all levels, ranging from the very simple *Water Lily*, with only fourteen templates, to the more challenging *Fire and Ice*, with sixty-two templates. There are also suggestions for borders, bindings, assembly, and quilting for when you're ready to finish your quilt.

Have fun and experiment with colors and prints new to you. It's playtime!

Water Lily, 1999, 16" × 18" (40 cm × 45 cm)

Water Lily

Try out this simple but pretty quilt pattern as a means of practicing the topstitch piecing appliqué technique and experimenting with color placement. There are just fourteen templates, so the pattern comes together surprisingly quickly.

DIMENSIONS
16″ × 18″ (40 cm × 45 cm) including borders and bindings

MATERIALS
Lily pad and dark bottom/side borders: scraps or ¼ yd (25 cm)
Background and light top/side borders: ½ yd (50 cm)
Stabilizer: 22″ × 22″ (55 cm × 55 cm)
Lily centers: ⅛″ (0.4 cm) yellow satin ribbon
Inner border: ¼ yd (25 cm)
Petals: scraps
Binding: ¼ yd (25 cm)

Assemble the templates on pages 116–117 as described for *Spring Tulip* on pages 4–11. These additional guidelines will help you plan your quilt.

• For the lily pad, choose fabric for template 11 that is a little lighter than the fabric for 13. Use at least three values of color for the flower petals. Petals 3 and 7 should be darker than the others to give the illusion of depth.

• Make the lily centers from loops of narrow satin ribbon or any ribbon that frays easily. Stitch down the ribbon at the base of template 7 before you put 9 in place. Likewise, attach ribbon to the base of template 3 before you pin down 10. Once the ribbon is secure, trim and fray it.

Make a double border as shown on page 52. The inner border should be the color of the flower to enhance it. For the same reason, choose a background fabric that has a hint of the flower color in it to echo the color and heighten the effect. Cut the inner border at 3″ (7.6 cm), fold it in half, press it, and stitch it to the design. Miter the corners if you wish, using the simple instructions on page 50. Stitch on the large border crooked for a unique effect. Cut the large border at 3½″ (9 cm). Mark it, turn it under, and press a ½″ (1.5 cm) seam allowance. Stitch the border at a slanted angle, leaving from ½″ to 1″ (1.5 cm to 2.5 cm) showing on the inner border. Measuring out from the straight top of the inner border, trim and square the project to a rectangle.

Sandwich and finish quilt as desired or use water motif (see page 75). Bind with French appliqué binding (see pages 58–59).

Analyzing the Templates

To help you choose colors for your fabrics, here's how the pattern is made up.

Background: templates 1, 2, 4, 6, 8, 12, 14
Lily pad: templates 11, 13
Petals: templates 3, 5, 7, 9, 10

Fabric Requirements

All patterns require stabilizer, and eventually, batting and backing to fit the project size. The yardage estimates for the quilt top patterns that follow are based on the projects as I created them. In many cases, the total size given includes borders and background. You may choose to use fewer or more fabrics in your work or enlarge the pattern. If so, adjust the yardage accordingly. If in doubt, buy a bit more of the fabric—a nice affirmation for a quilter, don't you think?

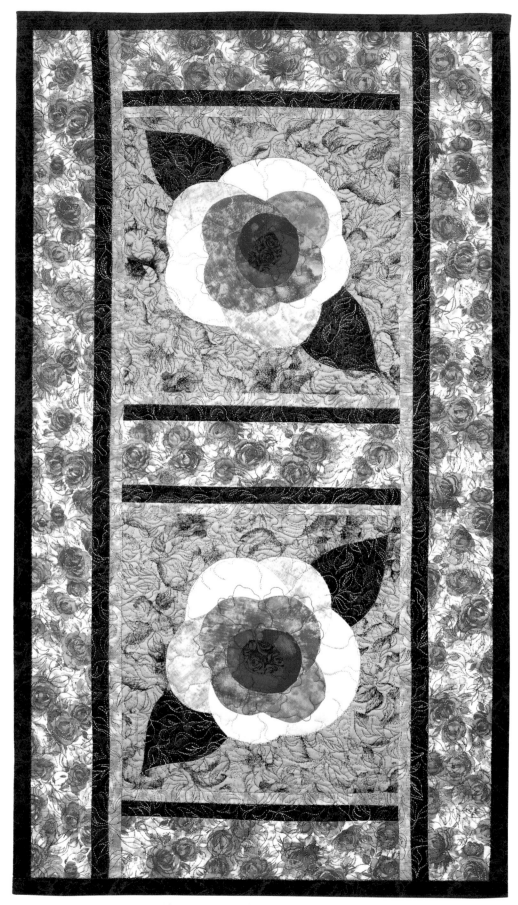

Cabbage Rose, 1999, 19¾″ × 35¼″ (49.3 cm × 88 cm)

Cabbage Rose

Don't be surprised if you catch a whiff of fragrant perfume from my cabbage rose as you make this fun and versatile pattern. The two-block runner is the perfect summertime table centerpiece.

DIMENSIONS
Each block: 10¼″ × 10¼″ (26 cm × 26 cm)
Runner: 19¾″ × 35¼″ (49.3 cm × 88 cm)

MATERIALS
Border: ½ yd (50 cm)
Green binding, sashing, and leaves: ⅔ yd (60 cm)
Background: ½ yd (50 cm)
Pink sashing: ¼ yd (25 cm)
Rose petals: scraps
Stabilizer: 40″ × 24″ (100 cm × 60 cm)

Assemble the templates on pages 118–119 as described for *Spring Tulip* on pages 4–11. These additional guidelines will help you plan your quilt.

• For the rose petals, use seven or eight gradations of the desired color for the best contrast. Remember, many times you can use the reverse of your fabric as a gradation.

• For the sashing, use one of the colors in the rose petals to enhance the flower. This two-block table runner has double sashing: the pink sashing is ½″ (1.5 cm) and the green sashing is ¾″ (2 cm). To construct pink and green sashing, follow directions for double borders (page 52). To construct floral borders, refer to "Straight Topstitch Borders" on page 49.

The borders can be any width you desire. On this table runner, they are 2¾″ (7 cm). Don't forget to add 1″ (2.5 cm) to the desired width for seam allowances.

Sandwich and quilt this table runner using free-motion stitching in the leaf design as discussed on page 74. Bind using ¾″ (2 cm) from French appliqué binding (see pages 58–59).

As a variation, you can use this pattern as a single block for a pillow cover or combine as many blocks as you wish to make a quilt, adding appropriate sashing and borders.

Analyzing the Templates

To help you choose colors for your fabrics, here's how the pattern is made up.

Background: templates 16, 17
Leaves: templates 14, 15
Rose petals: templates 1, 2, 3, 4, 5, 6, 7, 8, 9, 10, 11, 12, 13

Dogwood, 1998, 16″ × 20″ (40 cm × 50 cm)

Dogwood

This fun pattern with an Asian flair is a great way to try your hand at wrinkling and stuffing techniques to give your project texture, interest, and dimension.

DIMENSIONS

16″ × 20″ (40 cm × 50 cm) including borders and bindings

MATERIALS

Background: ½ yd (50 cm)
Inner border: ¼ yd (25 cm)
Binding: ¼ yd (25 cm)
Flower centers, petals, leaves, and branches: scraps
Border: ¼ yd (25 cm)
Stabilizer: 24″ × 24″ (60 cm × 60 cm)

Assemble the templates on pages 120–123 as described for *Spring Tulip* on pages 4–11. These additional guidelines will help you plan your quilt.

• Consider batik blue and green background fabrics that give the illusion of leaves and sky. But be sure that you have enough value contrast in the individual leaves or they'll blend in with the background.

• Use the wrinkling technique described on pages 35–36 on some of the petals (6, 7, 14, and 18).

• To stuff the flower centers or the foreground tree branch (13) trapunto-style, use the padded appliqué method described on pages 34–35. The inner border is ½″ (1.25 cm) (refer to page 52, "Double Borders").

To finish the quilt, sandwich the quilt top. Do not trim the stabilizer. The fabric for the backing and the batting should extend 4″ (10 cm) beyond the inner border. Quilt as desired, or use the leaf motif (refer to page 74).

Press well. On the quilt's surface, measure outward 2½″ (6.25 cm) from the fold of the inner border, drawing a straight line with the quilt marking pencil on all four sides to form a rectangle. Make sure the corners are square (90 degrees). Trim on the marked line with a rotary cutter and mat.

Cut four combination border/binding strips 4″ (10 cm) wide. Construct according to "Straight Border" directions (refer to pages 49–51). Turn the excess seam allowance of the border/binding fabric to the backside, turn under raw edges, and whipstitch to backing.

Analyzing the Templates

To help you choose colors for your fabrics, here's how the pattern is made up.

Background: templates 4, 5, 9, 12, 17, 21, 22, 26, 29, 32
Leaves: templates 8, 11, 15, 23, 27, 28, 30
Branches: templates 10, 13, 24, 25, 31
Petals: templates 2, 3, 6, 7, 14, 16, 18, 20
Flower centers: templates 1 and 19

Winds of Autumn, 1996, 14½″ × 15⅜″ (36.25 cm × 38.5 cm)

Winds of Autumn

Celebrate the most colorful season of the year with this easy quilt top. There are five different leaves waiting to challenge your creativity. There is no top or bottom to this design—it looks great no matter which side is up!

DIMENSIONS
$14\frac{1}{2}'' \times 15\frac{3}{8}''$ (36.25 cm × 38.5 cm)

MATERIALS
Background: $\frac{1}{3}$ yd (30 cm) or scraps
Border/binding: $\frac{1}{3}$ yd (30 cm)
Leaves: scraps
Stabilizer: 20″ × 20″ (50 cm × 50 cm)

Assemble the templates on pages 124–127 and as described for *Spring Tulip* on pages 4–11. These additional guidelines will help you build your quilt.

• For the background, try blending a variety of dark fabrics, or use fabric that simulates wind or rain and has a moody feel to it. Avoid fabrics that are too busy and will distract from your leaves (the focal point).

• For the leaves, use fabric scraps of any colors you wish. Choose colors that are vivid and bright. Vary the contrast of value (light to dark) among the five leaves. Templates 3 and 5 make up one leaf. They can be the same fabric, or template 5 can be a bit lighter for depth. Templates 17 and 18 also make up one leaf. Use darker fabric for 17 for the illusion that the leaf is curled.

To complete the quilt top, use the contoured-border technique as described in Steps 1 to 9 on pages 48–49 to create a border. As shown, quilt has a $1\frac{1}{2}''$ (3.75 cm) border. You may enlarge border width to $2\frac{1}{2}''$ (6.25 cm) if desired. Bind with French appliqué binding (see pages 58–59).

Analyzing the Templates

To help you choose colors for your fabrics, here's how the pattern is made up.

Background: templates 1, 2, 4, 6, 7, 8, 10, 11, 13, 14, 16, 19, 20, 21, 22
Leaves: templates 3, 5, 9, 12, 15, 17, 18

Fire and Ice #2, 2000, 14″ × 16¾″ (35 cm × 42 cm)

Fire and Ice #2

Although this pattern appears daunting, it is not difficult. It does, however, take time to construct because of the number of templates. Enlarge the pattern on an oversized (blueprint) copy machine to any size you desire. This pattern, with its sixty-two pieces, will help you use up some of the odds-and-ends scraps in your stash. This pattern is a smaller and simpler version of my quilt.

DIMENSIONS
14″ × 16¾″ (35 cm × 42 cm)

MATERIALS
Fire, icicles, separation, and embers: scraps
Stabilizer: 20″ × 20″ (50 cm × 50 cm) as shown or as needed if pattern
    is enlarged

Assemble the templates on pages 128–131 as described for *Spring Tulip* on pages 4–11. These additional guidelines will help you plan your quilt.

  • Use a strong value contrast in color. Vary the colors and values among the icicles and the flames. Using fabrics with little contrast for adjoining templates will give the illusion that two templates are one instead of separate pieces. You need color and value contrast within the design for it to be visually effective. The focal points are the flames and icicles. The dark bed of embers on the bottom and the dark area in the middle that separates the fire from the ice enhances both focal points.

  • Keep an open mind and palette. Use lavender, aqua, light green, pink, and other pastels for the ice as well as blue. For the fire, use bright magenta, coral, and gold as well as a variety of red, orange, and yellow. For the dark separation between the fire and ice, use navy, deep purple, or any other dark color instead of (or in addition to) black. Dark fabric imprinted with touches of red or a warm color will give the illusion of sparks flying.

  • Tuck under the points! Sometimes while pinning a prepared fabric template back into its space, you'll find that the seam allowance of a template point sticks out of place from the design. Simply turn under the protruding point and tuck it beneath the fabric template so that the succeeding template will cover it.

    Sandwich and quilt using flame stitch for fire (see page 75) and geometrics stitch for ice (see page 75). Finish using fast borderless finish (see page 48).

Analyzing the Templates

To help you choose colors for your fabrics, here's how the pattern is made up.

Fire: templates 4, 6, 7, 14, 21, 27, 28, 29, 30, 35, 40, 43, 46, 50, 52, 53, 56, 61, 62

Icicles: templates 1, 2, 3, 10, 11, 13, 15, 16, 19, 23, 24, 25, 37, 38, 39, 41, 42, 44, 45, 55, 58, 59

Dark separation between ice and fire: templates 9, 12, 17, 18, 20, 22, 26, 31, 33, 34, 36, 47, 48, 49, 54, 57

Embers: templates 5, 8, 27, 32, 51, 60

Feelin' Groovy, 1995, 53" × 55" (132 cm × 137 cm)

Feelin' Groovy

This whimsical pattern was based on the back art of my quilt *Blacklick Pond: Reflections at Twilight* (see page viii). This pattern is always a hit with frog lovers!

DIMENSIONS
Pattern only: $17^{3}/_{8}$" × $20^{3}/_{8}$" (43.5 cm × 50.5 cm)

MATERIALS
Green frog: ¼ yd (22.5 cm)
Pale green frog: ¼ yd (22.5 cm)
Dark lily pad: ⅓ yd (30 cm)
Light lily pad: scraps
Patchwork background: scraps
Eyes and mouth: scraps
Stabilizer: 24" × 24" (60 cm × 60 cm)

Assemble the templates on pages 132–137 as described below.
These additional guidelines will help you plan your quilt.

• Both the frog and lily pad are green, so take care to keep value contrast in your work. The green fabrics used in the lily pad may have a yellow tinge in them to set them apart from the frog's body. The background templates simulate a patchwork pond. Use a variety of fabrics that complement the frog.

• For the frog, templates 1, 5, 6, 8, 9, 12, and 16 are dark, intense green. Templates 2, 4, 7, 11, and 15 are pale green. Template 3 is black.

• For the lily pad, templates 10, 13, 14, 17, and 19 should be medium green, all the same fabric. Template 20 is light green.

• For the eyes, template A is black; B and C are pale green; and D and E are dark green; and F is white.

1. Trace the pattern onto freezer paper and pin it to the stabilizer. Include the eye socket holes, but do not trace templates A through F on the main pattern. Trace and piece the eyes separately. Cut out freezer-paper template 1 and carefully cut out the eyeholes from the paper before pressing it to the fabric. Cut a circular hole in the exposed fabric, leaving ample seam allowance to turn under. Use deep and frequent clips to assure that the eye socket hole turns under smoothly. Press to secure creases and set aside the template.

2. Each eye has six templates, and although tiny, they are easy to piece using the topstitch piecing technique. Trace eye templates A through F on a large piece of freezer paper. You'll need to position seam

Analyzing the Templates

To help you choose colors for your fabrics, here's how the pattern is made up.

Background: templates 18, 21, 22, 23, 24, 25, 26, 27, 28, 29, 30, 31, 32, 33, 34, 35
Frog: templates 1, 2, 3, 4, 5, 6, 7, 8, 9, 11, 12, 15, 16
Lily pad: templates 10, 13, 14, 17, 19, 20
Eyes: templates A, B, C, D, E, F

Piece eyes separately on stabilizer; then position them beneath template 1.

A = Black
B and C = Pale green
D and E = Intense green
F = white
Add star highlights to the eyes with white thread.

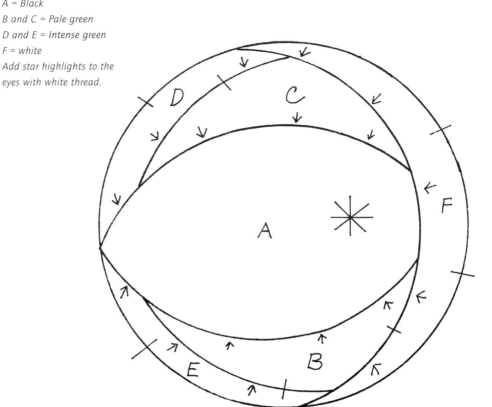

This enlarged, detailed illustration of the frog's eye will help you determine turned-under seam allowances and color placement.

allowances and move straight pins as you work. The extra paper gives you room to work and helps you maintain accuracy. Attach each traced freezer-paper eye to a separate piece of stabilizer. Piece and stitch both eyes at the same time, assembly-line fashion. There is no need to line the light-colored templates B, C, and F. Cut the seam allowance wider than the template so that when it is clipped and turned under, it will act as a lining to prevent shadowing. Blindstitch templates B and C to A. Continue with the rest of the templates. Press.

3. If you own a sewing machine with decorative stitches, you may add a white highlight at this point to the black part of the eye. For smoother machine stitching, add another small piece of stabilizer to the back of the eye. If you choose to embroider the eye highlights by hand, you will not need to add extra stabilizer. Position the highlight at the same place in each eye.

4. Correctly position each eye beneath the socket holes of template 1 and stitch in place.

Sandwich and quilt as desired. Add a hanging sleeve (refer to page 55). Bind with French appliqué binding (refer to pages 58–59) or try extending the pattern of the patchwork background into the binding (refer to page 64, "Extending Patterns into Quilt Binding").

Spiral Daisy

This is a very versatile pattern design. It can be "read" at least three ways. Plus there are countless exciting variations to this pattern depending on fabric placement and style. The drawings here suggest three ways to use color when piecing together the templates. When making a curved design like this, it's easier to piece concave (inside) curves. Begin with a concave edge and the templates will fall in place easily.

DIMENSIONS

17½" × 14" (43.75 cm × 35 cm) oval

MATERIALS

Petals: ½ yd (45 cm)
Background: ½ yd (45 cm)
Center circle: scrap at least 6" (15 cm) in diameter
Stabilizer: 20" × 20" (50 cm × 50 cm)

Note: For the *Spiral Pinwheel* and *Straight-Line Spiral* versions of this pattern, there are only thirteen templates each. In the photograph shown I have alternated five fabrics. You can alternate three very easily also. Fabric requirements about ¾ yd (70 cm) total for the surface, divided among the number of fabrics you choose.

Assemble the templates on pages 138–139 as described.

1. Trace the pattern onto freezer paper.
2. Carefully cut out freezer-paper center circle on seam line and set it aside. Pin freezer paper to stabilizer foundation. As you make each template, use a quilting pencil to lightly mark the center circle line and oval borderline on fabric as a placement guide. Leave a fabric allowance of about 1" (2.5 cm) to extend beyond oval borderline.
3. Turn under seam allowance for template 1. It overlaps the raw edges of the last template. Pin it to hold the crease, but do not sew it until the last template is in place.
4. Piece and blindstitch the remaining templates in order, referring back to directions for *Spring Tulip* on pages 4–11 if necessary. Prepare and pin a section of five or six templates before stitching. Press well after you sew each section. For accuracy, when you prepare next to last template, leave the freezer paper on until you pin the last template in place. Then remove the paper from both templates.
5. Avoid shadowing through the light-colored petals by leaving a seam allowance of at least the width of

To help you choose colors for your fabrics, here's how the pattern is made up for the *Spiral Daisy* version only.

Background: templates 2, 4, 6, 8, 10, 12, 14, 16, 18, 20, 22, 24
Petals: templates 1, 3, 5, 7, 9, 11, 13, 15, 17, 19, 21, 23
Center: template 25

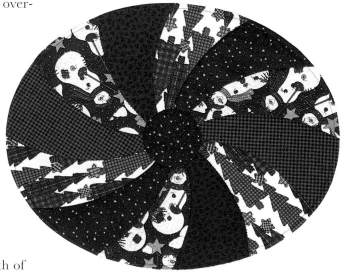

Use whimsical fabrics to create easy holiday gifts. I made this centerpiece as a gift for my sister.

Spiral Daisy, 1999, 17½″ × 14″ (43.75 cm × 35 cm) oval

the petal template—about 2″ (5 cm)—only on the straight side of the template. When the seam is turned under, it acts as a lining.

6. Trace the oval borderline (but no templates) from the pattern again on another sheet of freezer paper and cut it out. Center the freezer-paper oval on the surface of the quilt top, using the pencil markings you made on the fabric as a guide. Press well with a hot iron to adhere paper to top. Use a few pins for added security. Stitch completely around the circumference of the oval, using the paper edge as a guide for accuracy.

7. Remove the freezer paper and place it on the right side of the backing material. Cut out the back for the quilt, leaving a generous seam allowance. Remove the freezer paper and set it aside.

8. Place the backing right side up on an ample piece of batting and smooth out any wrinkles. Cut the batting to match the shape of the backing fabric. Press. Align constructed top surface face down on backing fabric, right sides together. Sandwich the project in this order: bottom, batting; middle, backing right side up; top, quilt top right side down, with the underside of the stabilizer facing you.

9. Center the freezer-paper oval on the top layer of the sandwich, using the stitched line as a guide. Press with the iron and pin all layers together. Stitch all layers, again using the edge of the freezer paper as a guide. Try to sew the entire circumference in one continuous motion for a smooth look.

10. Remove the pins and paper, and trim off the excess fabric and batting. Leave a ³⁄₈″ (1 cm) seam allowance. There is no fabric in the center circle, only stabilizer. Use scissors to cut wedge-shaped slits from the center of the circle out toward the fabric. Take care not to cut the backing fabric or any templates. You'll turn the quilt inside out through this hole. Don't make the slits any deeper than you need to, and don't cut beyond the outside line for the circle.

11. Carefully turn quilt inside out. Reach inside the hole with your hand or a blunt tool to adjust and even out the curved line of the seam so the project lies flat. Press well.

12. Topstitch ¼″ (0.75 cm) from the edge and quilt along the seams of the template lines from the outside edge to the center. Pull the bobbin thread tail to the surface before you begin stitching. Match the color of the bobbin thread to the backing fabric. Don't stitch beyond the pencil mark you made for the center circle (it will show on the backside). Once the stitching is complete, press well.

13. Iron the freezer-paper center circle to a heavy piece of cardboard and cut it out on the line as smoothly as possible. Remove the freezer paper. Place the cardboard circle on the wrong side of the fabric you've chosen for this template. Cut out a fabric circle, leaving 1″ (2.5 cm) allowance all around the cardboard. With a needle and heavy thread, baste around the outer edge of the fabric leaving long thread tails at the beginning and end. Pull the tails so that the fabric gathers around the cardboard circle. You want the tension to be taut, but not so much that the circle is distorted. Twist the tails, but don't tie them. Press very well on both sides with a hot iron to set the creases. Loosen the tails and remove the cardboard, disturbing fabric creases as little as possible. Center and pin the circle to the quilt according to your pencil markings and blindstitch it in place. Keep the cardboard template; you can use it every time you make this pattern.

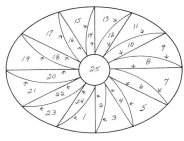

Spiral Daisy

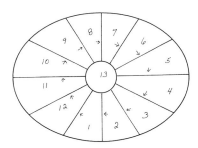

Straight-Line Spiral

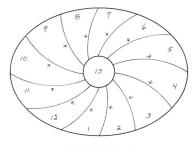

Spiral Pinwheel

Fire Within, 1998, 62½″ × 64″ (158 cm × 162 cm), cotton.

I believe that each of us burns with a spirit of creativity—very special gifts and talents given to us by our creator. This quilt depicts this burning creativity as a spiral. Our gifts and talents are the flames that radiate from our inner beings and touch the lives of others. The spiral and many of the flames are multidimensional, as are we, and rise from the quilt surface. Some flames twist, turn, and even move beyond the border of the quilt, showing that our ability to affect others is boundless.

Three-Dimensional Effects

*O*nce you have become familiar with the topstitch piecing technique and have tried one or more of the patterns in Chapter 2, you are ready to discover just how versatile this style of quiltmaking really is. You can achieve some very exciting effects that will make your quilts unique. Unlike with other quiltmaking styles, with topstitch piecing appliqué it is easy to manipulate the fabrics as you work. You have endless opportunities to change colors, textures, and even the dimensions of your quilt as it progresses.

While I work, I've developed the habit of asking myself, "Now, what would happen if? . . ." In this chapter, I will share with you some of the wonderful discoveries this simple question has led me to.

Padded Appliqué

Padded appliqué is best described as a very easy version of the old favorite trapunto. Leaves, flowers, rivulets of water, tree branches or trunks, stars, sky, or any other segment of a quilt design can be stuffed trapunto-style to give additional dimension, texture, and depth.

Padded appliqué is exceptionally easy. Begin with the completed quilt top (constructed on the stabilizer foundation) neatly pressed.

1. Determine which templates you want to be padded. Mark those templates with straight pins as a reference and a reminder.

2. Turn the quilt top over so the stabilizer faces up.

3. The straight pins indicate the templates you've chosen to pad. With a seam ripper, carefully make a straight cut into the stabilizer just large enough to maneuver the filling. Take care *not to cut the fabric* on the surface of the quilt.

4. Carefully stuff the template with small amounts of polyester fiberfill (loose filler used in craft projects) or scraps of batting. If you use batting, pull it apart and work with small pieces. Distribute it uniformly into the corners, sides, and body of the template. Use long-nosed serger tweezers to help you reach into the corners. Keep the padding light, since too much will pull at the seams on the quilt, making the quilt top look taut. It can also be a challenge to quilt through, even by machine.

5. To close the slit opening, simply insert a piece of webbing cut from a roll of fusible web and place it inside the slit between the padding and the stabilizer. Hold the two stabilizer edges together as best you can without burning your fingers and press it with an iron to fuse. When fusing, use a press cloth between the iron and the stabilizer to protect the soleplate of your iron. The fused webbing will hold the padding in place until the pattern is sandwiched

Step 3. Use a seam ripper to make a small slit in the stabilizer.

Step 4. Use long-nosed tweezers to distribute the padding evenly into the body, sides, and corners of the template. Don't overpad.

Step 5. Use a small piece of fusible web to close slit in stabilizer.

Windswept, 1999, 8" × 10½" (20 cm × 27 cm).
Don't overquilt padded templates. You'll flatten the areas you are trying to highlight. If, as here, the template you chose to pad is a light color in value, causing the seam from a darker neighboring template to shadow through in places, manipulate the padding between the light-colored fabric and the dark seam to fix the problem.

with batting and backing, and quilted. If you prefer, close the opening by hand using a whipstitch.

Avoid overquilting the areas you have padded. It will flatten and diminish the very effects you are trying to achieve. Use just enough quilting to anchor the padding in place so it will not shift.

Padded appliqué gives your quilt an exciting visual effect by adding contour and height to areas you want to accentuate. You can use it for a trapunto-style effect or in conjuction with other techniques, such as wrinkling, described below. This achieves even greater dimension and depth.

Wrinkling

Unlike padded appliqué, which is done once the quilt top is complete, *wrinkling* is a technique that takes place while you piece the top. Quite simply, before you cut the templates, you manipulate the fabric by hand, or wrinkle it, adding depth and texture to the quilt top. Wrinkling solid or small-print fabrics is an excellent way to alter their appearance for a fresh new look.

1. Determine which templates you want to be wrinkled and choose the fabric, but do not cut it yet. Lay the fabric right side up on the ironing board. Lightly dampen the fabric with water from a mist sprayer.

After the Storm detail. See full quilt on page 101.

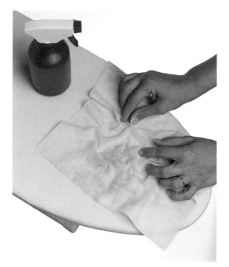

Step 2. Mist the fabric with water and arrange the wrinkles with your fingers.

Step 3. Set the wrinkles into the fabric by pressing them with hot iron.

Step 4. Press the freezer-paper template on the wrinkled fabric and then prepare as usual.

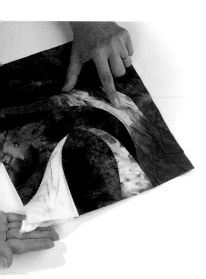

Step 7. Leave the crinkled template as is for a simple texture or pad it for a dimensional effect.

2. Arrange creases and folds in the material with your fingers. For optimum results and a smoother seam line, manipulate the fabric so the majority of the wrinkles are in the main body of the template. Try to avoid wrinkles on the edges where the seam allowance is turned under, which would cause a jagged look on the seam. Do not be concerned about the wrinkles on the other edges of the template. They will be flattened by the smooth stitching lines of succeeding templates.

3. Set the wrinkles in the fabric by pressing well with a hot iron until the dampness is gone.

4. Place the freezer-paper template on the fabric and cut it out. Turn under the designated seam allowance(s), clip the inward curves, and press as usual, tucking under all edges of the wrinkles as flat and smooth as possible.

5. Securely pin the template back into place on the quilt stabilizer so the wrinkles do not shift or move before you stitch down the template. I usually do not remove the freezer paper on the wrinkled template until after I pin the next template on top of it. This helps the wrinkles stay in place a little better.

6. Stitch as usual, using a machine blindstitch.

7. After you complete the entire quilt top, pad the wrinkled template from the back as with the padded appliqué technique (see pages 34–35). Alternatively, simply leave the wrinkled template as it is, textured but flat.

You may rearrange the wrinkles to suit your fancy and get as much height or dimension as desired. To do so, remoisten the wrinkles and iron them over again in different positions. During the quilting process, you may manipulate the wrinkles with your fingers and stitch them down in different or reversed directions for a novel look, or stitch along either or both sides of the wrinkle to get it to stand up from the surface. As with padded appliqué, don't overquilt, or you'll lose the dimensional effect.

Sculptured Appliqué

Sculptured appliqué opens up a whole new and exciting world in quilting to you. This extraordinary technique is a very effective way to give a three-dimensional quality to leaves, flower petals, water, or any other part of the design you may want to highlight. With sculptured appliqué, you first sew a freestanding template that includes three layers—a front surface fabric, a back surface fabric, and a center of stabilizer or flannel. The raw edge of the sculpted template is then sewn into the seams of the quilt top. The stabilizer or flannel adds stability and rigidity to the sculpted template, giving it the ability to stand up and off the surface of the quilt top. Sculptured appliqué is versatile. You can use it as a subtle accent or to create striking, freestanding shapes that turn and twist off the surface of the quilt. Either way, the result is eye-catching.

Sculptured appliqué allows you to accentuate sections of a pattern by making them three-dimensional. Begin by looking at the overall design and deciding which templates you want to emphasize. One way to approach this is to think of your fabrics in terms of color values and color contrasts. Dark colors recede; light colors advance. Thus if you add dimension to light colors in the pattern, you will add to the illusion that those parts of the pattern are in front of the dark-colored ones.

For example, look at *Red Maple Leaf* on page 38. Here, two different-colored fabrics—deep burgundy and light orange—combine to make the whole leaf. The curved line on the light fabric suggests that this part of the leaf curls over the top of the burgundy. It is the color choices that cause this visual illusion. Orange, a much lighter color value than burgundy, comes forward. Adding sculptured appliqué to this part of the leaf design will further enhance that effect.

Fire Within *detail. See full quilt on page 32.*

Covering the Ground Space

In this book's terms, *ground space* is the area that lies directly beneath a sculptured template on the surface of the quilt top. You must cover the stabilizer and other raw edges in the ground space area with fabric to provide a background for the freestanding sculptured template. You can cover the ground space in two ways:

- Construct the sculptured template twice. Construct the first version in the usual manner to cover the stabilizer (ground space). Construct the second version using the sculptured appliqué technique.
- Cut out the ground space template and the preceding template as one template, saving time, fabric, and an extra seam. You can use this method only if the fabric of the preceding template is suitable for the ground space.

Before you can choose the appropriate method for covering the ground space, first you must determine what part of the pattern it is.

Red Maple Leaf, 1999, 7¼″ × 6¼″ (18 cm × 15.6 cm)

Red Maple Leaf

To demonstrate sculptured appliqué, let's construct the *Red Maple Leaf* pattern, making just one of the templates (template 3) three-dimensional.

DIMENSIONS

$7^{1}/_{4}'' \times 6^{1}/_{4}''$ (18 cm $\times$ 15.6 cm)

MATERIALS

Use scraps for the background, leaves, and stabilizer
Stabilizer, batting, and backing

Assemble the templates on page 140 as described for *Spring Tulip* on pages 4–11 and in the steps below.

1. Template 1 is a background piece. Select a background fabric and cut it out, adding seam allowances all around. Do not turn under the seam allowances; they will be covered by subsequent templates. Pin background to stabilizer.

2. Cut out freezer-paper templates 2 and 3 *as a single unit.* Cut out the fabric template for 2 and 3, adding seam allowances all around, again as a single unit. The extra fabric cut with template 2 is the the ground space fabric that will sit beneath sculptured template 3. Turn under the seam allowance along the edge of template 2, indicated by small arrows. Pin it to the stabilizer and carefully remove the freezer paper. Blindstitch it in place. Cut freezer-paper template 3 from 2, saving 3 for the next step.

3. To make template 3 sculptured, assemble a sandwich of a stabilizer template and two fabric templates, cutting and stitching the template through all three layers. To begin, place a scrap of stabilizer larger than the template on the ironing board. On top of it place right side up a scrap of light fabric that will become the front surface of the leaf. On top of that, place right side down a dark fabric scrap that will become the underside of the leaf. In the photograph, I used the same dark fabric I used in Step 2. Place freezer-paper template 3 on top and press it onto the fabric sandwich with a hot iron. Pin the sandwich layers together so there is no shifting. Note that the fabric placed face up in the middle of the sandwich is the one that will be face up on the quilt top.

To help you choose colors for your fabrics, here's how the pattern is made up.

Background: templates 1, 4, 5, 6
Leaf: templates 2, 3

Fall photographs were the inspiration for Red Maple Leaf.

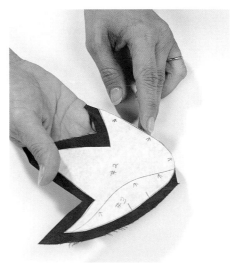

Step 2. Cut out templates 2 and 3 as one piece, turning under the seam allowance indicated.

Step 3. Layer with stabilizer at the bottom, top template fabric face up, then back template fabric face down, and then freezer-paper template face up on top.

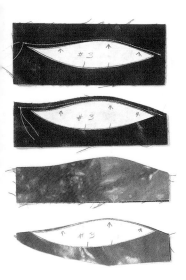

Steps 4–7. Stitch the outline along the indicated edge, about ⅛" (0.4 cm) from the edge of the freezer paper. Trim fabric. Turn the template right side out, adjusting and smoothing the seam. Match up the finished edge to the small arrows on the freezer-paper template. Press the freezer paper back onto the fabric.

Step 8a. Return template to the stabilizer foundation. It will be held in place by succeeding template 4.

Step 8b. The outer edge of the template is not stitched, giving it dimension.

4. Stitch through all layers along the edge indicated with small arrows. Stitch about ⅛" (0.4 cm) or slightly further from the edge of the freezer-paper template, depending on the thickness of the stabilizer and batting used. (When you turn the template inside out after stitching, you'll lose a little size, and incorporating this small extra margin makes up for the loss.)

5. Extend the line of stitching about ½" (1.5 cm) past both ends of the template. Trim the sandwich to ⅛" (0.4 cm) of the stitching.

6. Carefully clip any inward curves, if necessary. Remove the freezer-paper template. Turn the sandwich inside out so that the light fabric of the sculptured leaf is on top, the stabilizer is in the middle, and the dark fabric of the leaf's underside is underneath. Adjust and straighten the seam of the template. Press.

7. Iron the freezer paper back onto the leaf top fabric template, matching up the finished seam with the small arrows on the freezer-paper template.

8. Trim raw allowances around the freezer-paper template to approximately ½" (1.5 cm). Pin the template into its place on the stabilizer as usual. The finished, sewn seam on template 3 remains free—do not sew it down to the background.

9. Prepare background template 4 and fit it in place on the stabilizer foundation, covering the raw edges of sculptured template 3. Machine-blindstitch fabric template 4, taking extra care as you maneuver the presser foot over the added thickness of the preceding template.

10. Assemble templates 5 and 6 as usual.

There are two options to finish *Red Maple Leaf*:

1. Square the quilt top to 7" (17.5 cm). Add straight borders (see page 49). Sandwich the quilt top with lightweight batting and backing. Quilt as desired. Bind with French appliqué binding (pages 58–59).

2. Finish this quilt top by sandwiching the three layers in this order: (a) lightweight batting on the bottom; (b) backing fabric, right side up, on top of the batting; and (c) quilt top, face down, on top of the backing.

Flatten the layers and press. Pin the sandwich together to prevent shifting. Using a straight stitch, sew all around the outside edges of the quilt top, leaving an open 3″ (7.5 cm) gap in the middle of the fourth side. Instead of stitching straight border lines, try stitching in smooth, wavy curves to get the effect shown in the photograph. Trim all seams. Clip inside curves almost, but not quite, to the stitching line. Turn inside out through the 3″ (7.5 cm) opening and smooth the seam line. Press well to flatten. Topstitch ⅛″ (0.3 cm) around all edges. Whipstitch the opening by hand if it is not secured by the topstitching.

Helpful Hints

These pointers may help you with the sculptured appliqué technique.

• For easier handling while stitching the outline of large sculptured templates, trim the fabric sandwich to within 1½″ (4 cm) from any freezer-paper template edge.

• When stitching around the outline for a sculptured template with a narrow point (such as the tip of a flower petal), stitch a blunt line (2 to 3 stitches) across the tip instead of a sharp point. It improves and softens the look of the finished template.

• For a thicker, padded look, add thin batting or cotton flannel to the sculptured template. Place the padding on the bottom of the sandwich, beneath the stabilizer.

• Reduce the bulkiness from narrow points and the ends of sculptured templates by trimming away the stabilizer and other padding (such as batting or flannel) so they are not included in the points.

• After stitching the outline of a sculptured template, use extra long tweezers to aid in turning the template inside out; then use the tip to help smooth, adjust, and straighten the seam.

• Blindstitch the first cutting (ground space) of a template to the stabilizer foundation before pinning the sculptured cutting into place.

• When stitching down succeeding templates over the raw edges of sculptured templates, you might encounter small "humps," especially from the end points, due to the stabilizer or padding. If your sewing machine balks at the additional thickness, begin the stitching on the template in the area with the greatest bulk or density and sew toward the area with the least.

• The freestanding edge of a sculptured template is most often the side with the indicated turned-under seam allowance (small arrows) unless you decide otherwise. To give your sculptured template more freedom, you may outline stitch on several edges of the template, not just the one indicated by small arrows. Any template can be as free and/or sculptured as you like, as long as its raw edges are hidden or overlapped by another template.

Quilting a Sculptured Template

If a sculptured template is to be machine-quilted, you can do it before you pin it to the foundation and sew it in place. This is easier than quilting after the quilt top is complete.

For the best results with narrow points, stitch a blunt line across the tip and trim.

In a Mood, 1998, 14″ × 16¾″ (35 cm × 41.75 cm)

- Sometimes it's necessary to tack down the tip or a small portion of a freestanding template to hold it in place on the surface of the quilt. Use an invisible stitch (by hand) or a short length of blindstitch, or include a tiny area of the template in the free-motion quilting.

- You may combine the wrinkling technique described earlier in the chapter with sculptured appliqué for a textured, dimensional template. Remember, the middle fabric in the sandwich is the one to wrinkle.

Modifying One-Dimensional Block Designs

Using sculptured appliqué changes the texture and appearance of a quilt. Compare, for example, *In a Mood*, shown here, with *Spring Tulip* on page 2. Both use the same pattern, but this version employs the three-dimensional techniques of sculptured appliqué. You can add a little extra excitement to any traditional quilt block or any block of your own design by using sculptured appliqué.

This is how I used the pattern for *Spring Tulip* to create a three-dimensional quilt top, *In a Mood*, that pleased me even more than the original.

In a Mood

DIMENSIONS

14″ × 16¾″ (35 cm × 41.75 cm)
Tulip only: 9″ × 11½″ (22.5 cm × 28.75 cm)

MATERIALS

Tulip petals: scraps in four or five values of one color
Leaves: green scraps in 4 to 5 values
Background: ⅓ yd (30 cm)
Stabilizer: 20″ × 20″ (50 cm × 50 cm) lightweight

Using sculptured appliqué in your quilt lends texture and character.

Assemble the templates on pages 112–115 as described for *Spring Tulip* on pages 4–11 and in the steps below.

1. Template 2 is a foreground tulip petal and can be sculptured. Make the ground space beneath it (the first cutting of template 2) in a dark flower color to give the illusion there is another tulip petal beneath the sculptured one. Blindstitch ground space template 2 to the stabilizer foundation before proceeding with the sculptured cut of template 2.

2. Template 4 is the highlighted edge of a leaf and can be sculptured. The ground space beneath 4 is an extension of template 3, a shadowed area of the tulip leaf. Since both template 3 and the ground space for 4 can be made from the same dark green fabric, cut out freezer-paper templates 3 and 4 as one unit, turning under the seam allowance on all the edges with the small arrows (a portion of template 4 and all of 3). Return the template to the stabilizer foundation and blindstitch to anchor template 2. Continue with the second cut of template 4.

Step 4. To make a template almost completely freestanding, stitch around the freezer paper as shown, leaving enough area to turn the template right side out. Trim. Secure it in place and cover the raw edge with the seam of the next template.

3. Template 5 is a middleground petal and should be medium value in color. You may leave it as is or make it sculptured. If you decide to make 5 sculptured, use flower-colored fabric for the ground space beneath it to simulate another petal as you did with template 2. Choose fabric a shade lighter in color than you used for the ground space under 2. Stitch down to secure the remainder of freestanding template 2.

4. For sculptured template 5, you may choose either to limit the outline stitching to the side indicated by arrows or extend the stitching around the tip and upper left half of the petal to make it almost completely freestanding. Template 5 will be held in place by template 7.

5. Other templates that you can make sculptured are 14, 18 (combine freezer-paper templates 17 and 18 for the ground space), and 21 and 22 (combine freezer-paper templates 20, 21, and 22 for the ground space).

For a contoured inner border follow these guidelines:

• Using the *Spring Tulip* templates 25–28 on pages 112–115, trace the border design onto the freezer paper. Transfer all template markings including numbers, arrows indicating seams that will be turned under, and top of border. If the freezer paper is not big enough to accommodate the width of the border, overlap two sheets by 1″ (2.5 cm) and tape them together.

• With a pencil, mark ½″ (1.25 cm) from the inset's borderline into the body of the templates to create a second identically shaped but expanded inset borderline. You may find it helpful to use a flexible curve to do this. Align the flexible curve next to the inset borderline so that it follows the curves. Trace along the other side of the flexible curve with a pencil. The inner border formed will be approximately ½″ (1.25 cm) in width.

• Each of the four templates, 25–28, is now divided into two templates: a ½″ (1.25 cm) curved inner border template and a contoured corner border template approximately 2″ (5 cm) wide. Mark the inner border templates as 25a, 26a, 27a, and 28a, corresponding them to their parent templates. The little arrows that mark the seam allowances to be turned under are now on the inner border and are correct. The new inset borderline you created is the seam to be turned under for the contoured border templates. This seam will hide the raw edges of the inner border. Mark this seam with little arrows on templates 25–28.

• Refer to "Contoured Borders" (pages 48–49) and follow the general instructions beginning with the second step and the following modifications for the curved inner border:

　1. In Step 2, cut out the inset on the original borderline, leaving the inner border templates intact.

　2. In Step 4, construct the inner border template (25a) first, before proceeding with the contoured template (25). When you cut out the fabric templates for the inner border, leave seam allowances on all sides.

　3. In Step 6, the raw edge of template 28a is tucked under 25a.

In Review

In this chapter you've learned innovative techniques that not only change the surface texture, height, and shape of your quilts but will add intrigue and uniqueness. Plus they are just plain fun to do! Take time to play with these fabric manipulations. Incorporate padded appliqué, wrinkling, and sculptured appliqué into your work. Use your imagination! You will be amazed at how you can use the different creative special effects in your quilts.

Resting Place, 1999, 66½" × 87" (169 cm × 221 cm).

This quilt depicts the vastness and serenity of the Rocky Mountains. During a family hike, we stopped to rest at a beautiful site on the trail. Enamored with my surroundings, I was reluctant to leave. Even though many years have passed, I still feel as if part of my spirit, symbolized by the ribbon transparency, lovingly remains there. She is joyful and in total harmony with the mountains, water, and earth.

CHAPTER 4

Borders and Bindings

While I was developing the topstitch piecing technique, I experimented with unusual borders and bindings that I could construct in the same way as the rest of the quilt— on the surface. I liked working from the front of the project, where I could always see exactly what was going on. It allowed me to judge border and binding placement effortlessly.

In this chapter I share some exciting techniques that not only make adding borders and mitering corners easy but introduce some unusual effects that will make your quilt stand out. I also explain how I bind my quilts with a simple technique that allows the pattern of the quilt to flow into the binding for a perfect finish that is completely in tune with the overall look of the quilt.

Fast Borderless Finish

For a fast borderless finish:

1. Trim and square up the quilt top with a quilt marking pencil and include a ½" (1.5 cm) seam allowance measured out from the borderline on every side. Trim with a rotary cutter.

2. Cut the backing fabric and batting the same size as the quilt top (and allowances). Sandwich the project in this order: bottom, batting; middle, backing right side up; top, quilt top right side down. The right sides of the backing and quilt top must face, with the batting on the bottom. Match the edges and secure the sandwich with pins.

3. Stitch on all four sides, leaving a 5" (12.5 cm) opening on one side. Use a ½" (1.5 cm) seam allowance. Clip the corners, turn the sandwich inside out, adjust the seam opening to lie flat, and press.

4. Topstitch the quilt top ¼" (0.75 cm) from the edges, making sure to secure the open seam.

Contoured Borders

The *contoured-border technique* is a wonderful way to accentuate the lines or curves in a quilt pattern. Unlike traditional straight borders that rigidly frame your quilt inside a square, this technique allows you to mold the border around lines and shapes that occur at the edges of your quilt top pattern. You piece the border from four templates that each wrap around one corner of the quilt. There is no mitering to be done, so the border comes together quickly, easily, and accurately.

Here's how to create a contoured border for *Spring Tulip*, the quilt top we made in Chapter 1.

Note: Do not trim excess stabilizer from the quilt edges before adding the border. The stabilizer serves as a foundation for the border fabric.

DIMENSIONS
16¾" × 14" (35 cm × 42 cm)

MATERIALS
Border: ½ yd (45 cm) or scraps of four different fabrics
Batting: 20" × 20" (50 cm × 50 cm)
Backing: 20" × 20" (50 cm × 50 cm)

1. Using *Spring Tulip* templates 25 to 28 on pages 112–115, trace the border design onto freezer paper. Transfer all template markings, including numbers, arrows that indicate seams that will be turned under, and top of border. If the freezer paper is not big enough to accommodate the width of the border, overlap two sheets by about 1" (2.5 cm) and tape them together.

2. Cut the straight outer edges of the border freezer-paper templates. Carefully cut out the inset and set it aside. Do not cut the curved lines that separate each border piece yet. Lay the intact border over the quilt top, adjusting it until you are satisfied with exposed view of tulip, leaves, and background. Make sure no raw edges are visible.

3. Securely pin the border in place to avoid shifting. Realign the freezer-paper inset template inside the border and pin it to the quilt top. The inset acts as a guide to help you match up the edges of border templates.

4. Cut template 25 from the border. Iron the template to the right side of the border fabric. Using a quilt marking pencil and ruler, lightly mark the straight outer edges and the corner. (Later, when you square up and trim the quilt to the correct border size, these markings will be a rough guide.)

5. Cut fabric border template, adding ½" (1.5 cm) seam allowance on all curved sides. Allow a wider seam allowance, 1" (2.5 cm), for the straight outer edges. Turn under the seam allowance indicated by the small arrows and press. (Don't turn under the straight edges.) Position the fabric template on the quilt top, using the inset as a guide. Pin.

6. Repeat Steps 4 and 5 to cut and position the remaining three border templates. Neatly tuck the raw edge of template 28 underneath the turned-under seam allowance of template 25 and pin it in place.

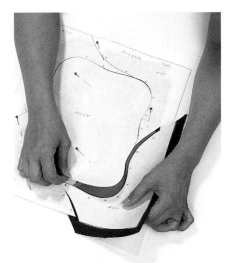

Step 2. Position border on the quilt top, centering it over the quilt pattern.

Step 3. Realign the inset inside the border template.

Step 5. Use the inset and neighboring border templates as a guide for matching up each border template.

7. Remove the freezer-paper inset template. Sew fabric border templates to the face of the quilt top with matching or blending thread, using a machine blindstitch.

8. Sandwich the quilt with a backing and batting. Machine- or hand-quilt it. Square up the outer edges and corners using the markings you made in Step 4 as a rough guide. Trim.

9. Create sewing lines for the binding on all four sides of the quilt. To do this, measure in ½″ (1.5 cm) from each outside edge. With a quilt marking pencil, draw a straight line on the quilt along the edge of a ruler. These sewing lines ensure a straight binding, and they are a helpful visual guide when sewing down the binding.

Straight Topstitch Borders

Once you have used topstitch piecing to make your quilt top, it's easy to keep going and use the same technique for the border. To do this, cut straight border strips with a rotary cutter and sew them down using a machine blindstitch onto the surface of the quilt top. As you will discover, mitering the corners is a snap.

1. Lay the quilt top on a flat surface. Even out all four sides using a quilter's square or ruler and quilt marking pencil. Draw straight lines at least ½″ (1.5 cm) in from all outer edges to form a perfect rectangle. This is your border stitching line. Do not cut quilt or stabilizer.

2. Decide how wide you would like your border to be. Add 1″ (2.5 cm) for seam allowances. Measure the quilt across the top, across the bottom, and from top to bottom on left and right sides to determine the border strip lengths you'll need to construct each side. If you plan to miter the corners, add double the width plus 2″ (5 cm) to each length measurement. This allows each border strip to

Perfect, Painless Mitering

Mitering borders and bindings has never been this easy for a quilter—no fuss, no frustration!

1. Draw a straight line across the top border strip from the inside corner to the outside corner where the two border strips cross. You can use the corner-to-corner method to accurately miter any corner, whatever the degree, in your quilts. With a 90-degree corner, use a quilting ruler with a 45-degree angle marking to check that the angle is correct.

2. Fold the top strip under along the marked pencil line and press. Trim away excess fabric from the top strip, leaving a ½" (1.5 cm) seam allowance from the fold line. Press down again, pin, and stitch the border in place.

3. If your border fabric wants to stretch while you're stitching, you might try using a walking foot or first stitch down the main part of the border to within an inch of each corner, then figure the angles, press, trim, and sew down the rest of the border.

4. Continue mitering the remaining corners of the quilt top.

Step 1. Use a ruler to draw a straight line from the inside corner of the border to the outside corner.

Step 2. Fold the top border strip under on the drawn line, trim the seam allowance, and pin easily to form a perfectly mitered corner.

Spring Tulip with an Amish Twist, 1998, 15" × 17¾" (38 cm × 44.3 cm)

overlap and extend at least 1″ (2.5 cm) beyond the border strips on either side of it. For a straight boxed border, measure the length of left and right sides, top, and bottom of quilt. Add 2″ (5 cm) to each of the short sides. Add double the border width plus 2″ (5 cm) to top and bottom measurements.

3. Cut border strips from the fabric using a rotary cutter. Cut fabric crosswise on the grain. This little extra stretch allows the border to hang straight. Borders cut parallel with selvage edges tend to curl once they are sewn down. Lay border strips right side up on table. Using a ruler and a sharp quilt marking pencil, draw a straight line ½″ (1.5 cm) in from the raw edge, along the outer long edge of each border strip.

Step 4. Use the marked line to position and pin a straight border to the quilt.

4. Turn under a ½″ (1.5 cm) seam allowance along the drawn line and press carefully with an iron. Using the marked pencil line already drawn on the quilt as a guide, carefully match the crease of the turned-under seam to the marked line. Borders are constructed and sewn from the top of the quilt. Attach the short borders first. You may either pin border strips in place or hold and sew strips directly to the quilt surface, matching crease to marked line as you stitch. Use a machine blindstitch with matching or blending thread to sew on borders. Press to flatten.

5. For a straight-edged border, use a ruler and quilt marking pencil to extend the marked stitching lines of the two remaining sides to include the borders you just attached. Pin the last two borders in place and stitch them down. If you plan to miter, do not pin down the corners.

Extending a Quilt Pattern into the Border

For an unusual and striking effect, you may extend the pattern of the quilt top's body into the border. Make the borders for the sides of the quilt top first. After you sew the side borders to the quilt top, continue with the top and bottom borders.

1. Figure the width and length measurements for the border. Decide how wide you want the border to be and add 1″ (2.5 cm) for seam allowances. (This figure is the total width.) Measure the side of the quilt top for length. For a straight-edged border, add 2″ (5 cm) to that measurement. If you plan to miter the corners, double the total width and add it to the length for the total length sum. For instance, if the total width figure is 3″ (7.5 cm), then add 6″ (15 cm) to the border length.

2. Using a rotary cutter and mat, cut a freezer-paper strip that is as wide as the total width and as long as the total length. At the same time, cut a strip of waxed paper to the same measurements. Set the waxed paper strip aside.

3. Use a ruler to measure a ½″ (1.25 cm) seam allowance along the top length of the freezer-paper strip, dull side up, and mark with pencil. Fold the freezer paper to the backside, along the marked seam allowance line.

4. Butt the fold of the freezer paper to the borderline of the quilt top, centering the length so it is equal on both sides. Pin to secure.

5. Design a template pattern for the border strip by using a flexible curve or ruler to extend or complete the pattern lines from the quilt top's body to the freezer paper border, marking it in pencil. Be very precise with the markings, especially at the fold, to allow for the border template to match up exactly with the quilt (see page 65 for illustrations). Mark each template with notes regarding color preferences or fabrics as you draw it. This organizational step helps you remember the template sequence and fabric you need to use during construction.

6. Open the freezer paper and use the ruler or flexible curve to complete the line markings you drew.

7. Pin the freezer-paper border to the waxed paper strip, matching the long edges. (The waxed paper acts as a foundation.) Pin well.

8. Construct templates as described in Chapter 1. Leave fabric seam allowances between the templates, but not along the outside edges. Do not cut the waxed paper while constructing templates. Leave the freezer paper on each template until you stitch it down. Blindstitch the templates together to form a fabric border strip. Remove the freezer paper and waxed paper from the border strip and press (see page 65 for illustrations).

9. Fold under the ½″ (1.25 cm) seam allowance along the top edge of the border strip and press. Align the border to the quilt top, matching the pattern lines of the border strip to the quilt body. Pin in place. Blindstitch the border to the quilt top. Press. Repeat steps 3 through 9 to construct the remaining borders.

10. With a ruler measure ½″ (1.25 cm) along the raw edge to determine the binding line and mark it. Finish with desired binding.

Double Borders

One of my favorite ways to border a quilt is to accentuate a focal point of the pattern by repeating the same fabric or the same color in a narrow inner border. In *Calla Lily*, the white border accentuates the flowers by drawing the eye to it. It also helps balance the overall color scheme. Here's how to make a narrow, ½″ (1.5 cm) inner border.

1. Prepare the quilt top as in Step 1 of "Straight Topstitch Borders" (page 49). Measure up the sides of the quilt as in Step 2. If you plan to miter the corners, do not forget to add extra length to overlap adjacent borders. Using a rotary cutter and mat, cut border fabric strips 2″ (5 cm) wide. Fold the strips in half lengthwise wrong sides together and press. Position the fold of the binding strip on the drawn borderline and pin in place.

2. Sew the narrow border down using a machine blindstitch and matching thread. Press. Square up the quilt. Measure ½″ (1.5 cm) outward from the sewn seam and draw a new borderline with a quilt marking pencil.

3. Add an outer border as in Steps 3 through 5 of "Straight Topstitch Borders."

Calla Lily, 1998, 15" × 17½" (38 cm × 44 cm)

Child's Play. **Back art on** ***After the Storm.*** **See front of quilt on page 101.**

This is a nostalgic look back to when I was younger and things were simpler. What I perceived as a difficulty
then is child's play compared to the problems I've encountered as I've grown older.

Adding Back Art to Your Quilt

Typically, quilts are backed with a single fabric. To add whimsy, enhance, or continue the theme of the quilt top, you can design a simple back art pattern to use as backing for your quilt. Back art gives the quilt a distinctive touch and completed look.

Here are some tips to help you add back art to your quilts:

- Keep the pattern simple. The back art should complement, not rival, the quilt top.
- Draw the pattern for back art on paper and piece it on the stabilizer in the same way as the quilt top.

Adding a Sleeve

After quilting, you may add a hanging sleeve to a quilt before you bind it. To construct a sleeve for the back of the quilt follow these simple steps:

1. Decide the width you want the sleeve to be. Add to that number the finished width the binding will be. Double that sum.

2. To calculate length, measure across the very top edge of the quilt. Subtract from that number the finished binding width multiplied by 4. For example, if the quilt measures 60″ across the top and the binding will be 1″, the final length is 60″ minus 4″ (4 × 1″), or 56″. (If the quilt measures 152 cm across the top and the binding will be 2.5 cm, the final length is 152 cm minus 10 cm [4 × 2.5], or 142 cm.)

3. Use a rotary cutter and mat to cut the sleeve fabric (usually the same as the backing fabric) in the width and length amounts you calculated.

4. Finish the raw edges on the short sides (width) by measuring and marking a 1″ (2.5 cm) seam allowance on each side. Fold on the marked line and use fusible web (from a roll) to fuse the raw edges to the wrong side of the fabric. On the right side, machine-topstitch ½″ to ¾″ (1.5 cm to 2 cm) from the crease with matching thread to secure the edge.

5. Fold the sleeve in half lengthwise with wrong sides together and edges matching. Press well.

6. Match the raw edges of the sleeve to the top edge of the quilt. Center the sleeve so that its edges lie equal distance from the quilt's side edges. Pin well both at the top of the sleeve and at the fold so the sleeve does not shift.

7. Machine-topstitch the sleeve to the top of the quilt between the binding line and the raw edge, and whipstitch the sleeve fold to the quilt backing.

- Plan your back art surface to be at least 4″ (10 cm) larger on every side than the quilt top. This allows margin for error and ease while sandwiching the quilt.
- If the shape of the quilt top is odd, asymmetrical, or multisided, use that same quilt shape *in reverse* as the shape for the back art surface.
- If your back art pattern has large templates, some fabric stretching may occur, especially if you cut the fabric template on the bias. After you prepare each large template, blindstitch it to the stabilizer and press it well before adding another template.
- To sandwich the quilt, layer as follows:
    1. Completed backing, centered and facedown on a table;
    2. batting on top of the backing; and
    3. the quilt top, centered and face up, on the top.
  Make sure the quilt top pattern and back art pattern are correctly aligned. Smooth all layers, and baste or pin sandwich together.
- Free-motion quilt or machine-quilt using a walking foot. The five layers in the quilt (in order, quilt top fabric, stabilizer, batting, stabilizer, and back art fabric) help rather than hinder free-motion stitching. The bulk stabilizes the stitching and helps to regulate the stitch tension. Note that the back art is not quilted before it is sandwiched with the quilt top.
- Add a hanging sleeve. Refer to "Extending Back Art Patterns into the Sleeve," page 56.
- Bind using French appliqué binding, page 58. Match the binding to the front of the quilt.

Extending Back Art Patterns into the Sleeve

Many of my quilts have patterns on the backside as well as the front. I need sleeves to hang the quilts but want continuity in the patterns, too. I use a variation of the technique for extending patterns into the quilt binding to incorporate my back art patterns into the quilt sleeve.

1. Quilt the project, but do not bind it. Decide how wide the sleeve should be and add the width of finished binding to that number.

2. Measure the sum down from the top edge of the quilt back. Measure and mark at least three times—on each side and in the center. Use a ruler and a quilt marking pencil or drafting tape to connect markings to form a straight line across the back of the quilt. Use this line instead of the binding line of Step 4 of

The Spirit and the Tree. Back of *Resting Place.* See front of quilt on page 46.

My spirit is wrapped around an evergreen tree. I have a special place in my heart for trees—they remind me of people. All are unique and have their own personalities. The old trees that have survived many of life's storms are stately, twisted, and gnarled, which adds to their beauty and character.

"Extending Quilt Patterns into the Quilt Binding" on pages 64–66. Butt the fold of the freezer paper against this line.

3. Cut the width of the freezer-paper strip twice as big as the measurement you just made. For length, refer to Step 2 on page 55 ("Adding a Sleeve"). Fold the freezer paper in half lengthwise and pin the fold to the line. Continue as in Steps 4 through 10 on pages 64 to 66.

4. Finish raw fabric edges on the sides of the sleeve as in Step 4 on page 55 ("Adding a Sleeve").

5. Fold pieced sleeve in half lengthwise, wrong sides together, and press. Place the fold of the sleeve on the marked line of the quilt. Adjust the sleeve to the quilt so that the extended pattern matches the pattern on the quilt. Securely pin the sleeve to the quilt at the fold as well as on the top edge of the quilt.

6. Machine-stitch the top of the sleeve to the top edge of the quilt (above the binding line) and whipstitch the fold to the quilt back.

Silhouette. Back art on *Tears on Blacklick Pond.* See front of quilt on page xviii.
The leaves have fallen and only the silhouette of a bare tree remains until spring. The blue borders represent the pond.

Width of Binding Strips

How wide should you cut binding strips? First, decide how wide you want the binding to appear on the front of the quilt. Multiply that number by 4. Add a 1½″ (4.5 cm) allowance for turning under the raw edges on the backside. For example, for a ½″ (1.5 cm) binding, cut binding strips that measure 3½″ (10.5 cm); for a ¾″ (2 cm) binding, cut strips that measure 4½″ (12.5 cm); and for a 1″ (2.5 cm) binding, cut strips that measure 5½″ (14.5 cm).

If you are making a binding for a thick quilt, you may wish to add a little bit extra width—an additional ½″ (1.5)—when cutting binding strips. This allows for a more generous binding to fold over the bulky edges.

French Appliqué Binding

French appliqué binding is an easier version of the traditional double-binding technique that is used on most quilts. To make a ½″ (1.5 cm) French appliqué binding, use the following guidelines.

1. With a quilt marking pencil, mark a trimmed and squared quilt top ½″ (1.5 cm) from the edge on all four sides. Use this line as a visual guide for stitching on the binding. (Note that these instructions are for ½″ [1.5 cm] binding. If you choose to make your binding a different width, for example 1″ [2.5 cm], then square the quilt top and measure 1″ [2.5 cm] from each edge.)

2. Cut binding fabric with a rotary cutter in 3½″ (10.5 cm) strips. To figure length, you must first decide whether or not to miter the binding corners. Mitering requires additional length for each side. Measure each side of the quilt top. If you intend to miter, add the width of the binding you figured, in this case 3½″ (10.5 cm), plus 2″ (5 cm). Do this for each side of the quilt. If your quilt is 20″ (50 cm), for instance, cut each strip 3½″ (10.5 cm) wide and 25½″ (65.5 cm) long. If you are making a straight boxed binding, measure left and right sides of quilt first. Add 2″ (5 cm) to each side measurement. Measure top and bottom of quilt. To each measurement, add the width plus 2″ (5 cm). In this case, your 20″ (50 cm) quilt will need two 22″ × 3½″ (55 cm × 10.5 cm) strips and two 25½″ × 3½″ (65.5 cm × 10.5 cm) strips.

3. Fold the binding strips in half lengthwise, wrong sides together. Press carefully.

4. Add left and right side strips first. Position the binding on the quilt surface with the fold aligned on the ½″ (1.5 cm) seam allowance mark.

Step 4. Position the fold of the binding on the marked seam allowance. Pin and sew the binding on the surface of the quilt with a machine-blindstitch.

Step 6. Extend the top binding line to include the left and right side bindings. Sew down the top binding strip on the drawn line.

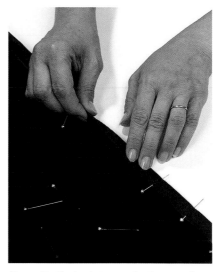

Step 7. On the back, turn under the raw edges of the binding and whipstitch.

Crosswise Grain Binding Strips

I recommend cutting binding strips on the crosswise grain of the fabric. Crosswise grain (widthwise) runs perpendicular to the selvage (lengthwise) edges of the fabric. A crosswise grain binding has some stretch, lies flat on the quilt, and handles easily. If I am binding a quilt with lots of curves, such as a quilt with a scalloped effect, then I cut the binding from the fabric bias for maximum stretch. I do not recommend cutting a binding on the lengthwise (straight) grain. A binding cut on the straight edge has no stretch, and, in my experience, appears to be taut even when it is measured properly.

5. Pin a side binding strip to the quilt a little at a time, spacing pins about 1″ (2.5 cm) apart. Resist the urge to stitch without pinning; because the binding has some stretch, the tension will be uneven if you do. Stitch the binding to the quilt using a machine blindstitch. Press side binding strips flat.

6. For straight boxed corners, mark each of four corners using a ruler or square and quilt marking pencil, extending parallel ½″ (1.5 cm) binding lines on the top and bottom of the quilt top to include the new side binding strips. Sew down the top and bottom binding strips on top of the side binding strips, creating a 90-degree corner. For mitered corners, follow the directions for mitering on page 50.

7. After you've sewn on all four strips, square up the corners from the front and trim excess fabric from the seams at the corners on the backside to get rid of any extra bulk. Turn the quilt top over. Fold the binding over to the backside, turn under the raw edges, and whipstitch the binding to the quilt back.

Continuous French Appliqué Binding

With the continuous French appliqué binding method, you simply join the binding strips together into a continuous strip before sewing them onto the quilt top. The following directions are for a ½″ (1.5 cm) binding, but you can easily adjust the width to suit your quilt (see Step 1 of "French Appliqué Binding"). Photos appear on page 60.

1. Cut binding strips as in Step 2 of "French Appliqué Binding." Using a ruler and quilt marking pencil, draw a 45-degree angle on the right side of the fabric toward the end of a binding strip. Trim to ½″ (1.5 cm) from the drawn line. Fold under the seam allowance on the drawn line and press.

2. Place this first binding strip right side up and turned-under seam down on top of a second binding strip (fabric right side up) toward its end. Use a ruler or a rotary mat to help you align the top and bottom edges so they are straight. Pin the binding strip in place.

3. Machine-blindstitch the binding strip in place. Press the seam with an iron. Repeat with remaining binding strips. To give your continuous binding stability as you machine-blindstitch joining seams, place a small strip of waxed paper underneath the fabric before stitching the seams together. It acts as stabilizer, makes stitching easier, and rips away easily after sewing.

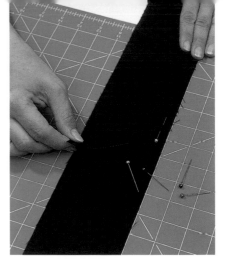

Step 1a. Use a ruler to mark a 45-degree angle on the continuous binding strip.

Step 1b. Trim to ½" (1.5 cm) of the drawn line and turn under the seam allowance.

Step 2. Align the first binding strip with the second one so that the top and bottom edges are straight. Pin.

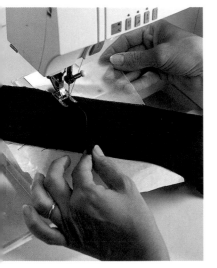

Step 3. Use waxed paper as a temporary stabilizer when stitching the seam of the binding.

Combination Border and Binding

This rather unusual method of adding binding is an extension of the technique for making contoured borders described on pages 48–49. It is a one-step method that allows you to bind as you border. Quite simply, to make a combination border and binding, you extend the outside edges of the border and wrap them to the back of the quilt, where you whipstitch them in place.

The amount you extend the border depends on the look you want. When you sew on this border, the bobbin stitches will show on the back. To hide these stitches, add more fabric. Otherwise, you'll need only enough fabric to turn to the backside, fold under, and whipstitch.

You can adopt this technique for any quilt or wall hanging. Let's practice with a combination border and binding for the *Spring Tulip* quilt top from Chapter 1. Note that unlike traditional borders, the combination border and binding is added *after* quilting.

DIMENSIONS
16¾" × 14" (42 cm × 35 cm)

MATERIALS
Border/binding: ½ yd (45 cm)
Batting: 20" × 20" (50 cm × 50 cm)
Backing: 20" × 20" (50 cm × 50 cm)

1. Prepare a quilt sandwich with batting and backing. Machine- or hand-quilt as desired and press.

2. As described in Step 1 of "Contoured Borders" on page 48, trace border templates 25 to 28 onto a large sheet of freezer paper. If you need more width, tape two sheets together. Center the drawing, allowing enough room to expand the pattern edges on all sides.

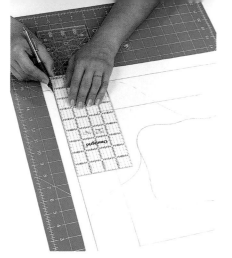

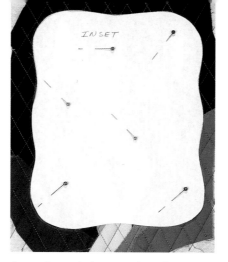

Step 3. Extend the width of the binding by adding to the existing borderline.

Step 4. Center the inset over the quilt pattern.

Step 5. Use a clear ruler to measure the desired surface width, starting from the outside curves. Form a rectangle.

3. To hide the stitches on the quilt back, use a clear quilting ruler to measure the distance from the inner curves of the contoured borderline to the straight edge of the pattern. To that measurement add 1″ (2.5 cm) for seam allowances. Now measure the sum (distance plus 1″/2.5 cm) outward from the pattern edge and mark, creating a new extended edge. Draw lines on all four sides, forming a rectangle. Square up the corners. If you simply want to extend the combination border and binding to the back of the quilt and are not concerned about hiding stitches, add 1″ (2.5 cm) to the existing borderline. Your drawing should look like a window with a curved inset.

4. Carefully cut out the freezer-paper inset, leaving the border template window intact. Center the freezer-paper inset on the surface of the quilt so the pattern is correctly positioned and there are no raw edges beneath the paper inset. Pin inset in place. Lightly mark the quilt around the entire curved edge of the freezer-paper inset with a quilt marking pencil. This is the borderline for the templates.

5. On the quilt top, use a quilter's clear ruler to measure the border width (the original measurement, not the expanded one) outward from the inner curves of the inset borderline and mark a line. Do this on all four sides to form a rectangle.

6. Square up the corners so the rectangle is even. Trim the quilt on the marked line, including foundation stabilizer and batting, with a rotary cutter. Position the freezer-paper border templates on the quilt top, using the freezer-paper inset as a guide. Pin it in place.

7. Prepare template 25 from the combination border and binding. Iron the template to the right side of the fabric. Cut the fabric, leaving ample seam allowances on the curved inside edges of the template. There is no need for seam allowances on straight outer edges. Turn under the seam indicated by small arrows and press in place. Position the fabric template in place on the quilt using freezer-paper template and inset as visual guides. Pin the fabric template in place through fabric, but not freezer paper.

Tightening a Border for a Better Fit

Sometimes, depending on the density of the quilting, a project will shrink when you quilt it, and the border from the prepared design may be too large and not fit correctly. If this happens, you need to tighten the border for a better fit. Simply make straight tucks in the freezer-paper border template, secure the tucks with drafting tape, and even out the borderline so the curves flow smoothly.

If the combination border and binding template is too large due to shrinkage during quilting, make straight tucks in it to make it fit.

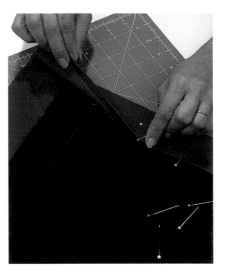

Step 7. The combination border and binding template is wider and extends beyond the quilt top.

Step 10. Adjust the size of the combination border and binding on the back to hide bobbin thread from the machine blindstitch. Turn under the raw edges.

8. Repeat Step 5 on page 48 to cut and position remaining three border pieces. Note that the raw edge of template 28 is neatly tucked underneath the turned-in seam allowance of template 25 and pinned in place. If the rectangular outer combination border and binding seems uneven or lopsided, use a quilter's square or ruler to help you even up the sides.

9. Remove the freezer-paper inset. Sew the templates to the surface of the quilt with matching or blending thread using a machine blindstitch. As you sew, you will run off the edge of the quilt and continue to stitch on a single layer of fabric. Take your time as you sew over the hump. If needed, put a piece of waxed paper beneath the fabric templates to give the stitches extra stability.

10. Turn the quilt face down. Fold the binding edges from the front of the quilt to the back, allowing for the correct binding width on the surface. Press. Use the excess fabric to form a border on the back, hiding the bobbin blind-stitches you made when you sewed the front border. Tuck the raw edges under and whipstitch the binding to the back of the quilt. If desired, add a sleeve (see page 55).

Binding Large Quilts

Squaring up large quilts can be a frustrating task. I've marked many quilt sides and corners where I thought the binding lines should be, only to find the lines did not measure up square. Often the lines were difficult, if not impossible, to remove from the quilt. Through experimentation, I've found the easiest way to square up large quilts and mark binding lines is to use drafting tape instead of marking pencils. Be forewarned, however: do not confuse drafting tape with

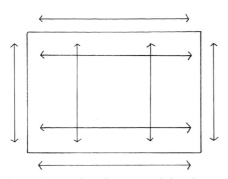

Step 1. Measure the quilt top several times in each direction until you get consistent measurements.

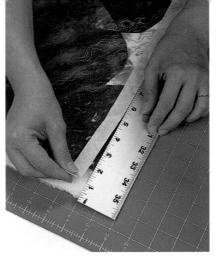

Step 3. Use drafting tape to mark the binding lines. You can lift and adjust the tape to make all sides correct, leaving no marks.

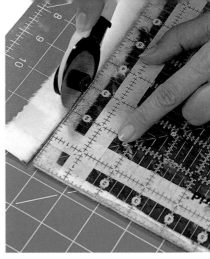

Step 4. Measuring from the outside edge of tape, trim the quilt top to the width of the binding.

common masking tape, even though they look the same. Masking tape will leave a residue and ruin your quilt. I've never had residue problems with drafting tape, but to be safe, test by taping it to fabric scraps and avoid ironing over the tape.

Here are the steps for squaring up and marking large quilts for binding:

1. Lay the quilt flat on a clean and uncluttered floor or on a large table. Use a metal tape measure to correctly measure equal distances from side to side and from top to bottom. Measure more than once in each direction across the length and width of the quilt. Insert straight pins to mark your measurements. Use a clear quilter's square to ensure each corner measures 90 degrees. Double-check all the measurements until you are satisfied they are accurate and the quilt sides are proportionate and symmetrical.

2. Line up a metal yardstick against the straight pins, using the pins as a guide to form a straight binding line. The ruler must be on the outside of the binding line, the side closest to the raw edges of the quilt.

Step 5. Use the outside edge of the tape to position the binding, and pin it securely.

3. Mark the quilt binding line using long strips of ³⁄₄″ (2 cm) drafting tape. Place the strips of tape against the inside edge of the binding line, toward the center of the quilt. The edge of the yardstick acts as a guide to keep the tape strips straight. As you put the tape in place, remove the pins from the quilt. Measure again for accuracy. If the binding lines still do not measure up correctly, lift and readjust the tape, as many times as necessary, with no quilt pencil markings to erase or to confuse you.

4. Once you have determined the desired width of the binding, use a clear ruler to measure that distance outward from the outside edge of the tape. Trim the raw edges of the quilt with a rotary cutter and the ruler.

5. Sew down the binding using the machine-blindstitch method described in Chapter 1 (pages 9–10). The outside edge of the tape is the binding line and acts as a visual guide to placement. The binding is positioned against the outside edge and pinned in place with straight pins. After the binding is pinned to the quilt, stitch the binding in place with a machine blindstitch, removing the tape as you go. Do not stitch on the tape. Make sure you remove the tape completely before ironing the quilt.

Extending Patterns into the Quilt Binding

There are times you may wish to extend the pattern from the body of the quilt into the binding for a look of continuity. The steps below describe the easiest way to assemble such a binding with precision. In summary, you will design a pattern for each binding strip and piece together the templates. You construct the quilt in four binding strips; you apply the strips first, and then sew down the top and bottom strips.

1. Decide how wide you want the binding to appear on the front of the quilt. Refer to page 58 to determine how wide to cut the strips.

2. Square up the quilt. Add a hanging sleeve if desired (see page 55). Mark the binding line, leaving enough raw edge on the trimmed quilt to equal the width of binding you want. Trim off the excess with a rotary cutter.

3. To begin, you will design a freezer-paper pattern for a side binding strip. It doesn't matter whether you begin on the right or the left side of the quilt. Cut a strip of freezer paper in the width you determined in Step 1. The length of this freezer-paper strip should equal the length of the side of the quilt plus 2″ (5 cm).

If you intend to miter the binding at the corners, allow enough extra length on all sides to accommodate miters (see Step 2 on page 49). Use a mat and rotary cutter (with an old blade rather than wasting a new one) to cut the freezer paper. It is easier to manage a long piece if you fold paper several times widthwise, matching edges exactly, before cutting it on the mat.

4. Carefully fold the freezer paper in half lengthwise, shiny sides together. Press the fold with your fingers and the side of a pencil to sharpen the crease. The folded freezer-paper strip should be longer than the side of your quilt. Center it lengthwise so that it equally overlaps the top and the bottom of the quilt. For placement widthwise, butt the fold of the freezer-paper strip against the binding line you marked on the side of the quilt. Be very exact. The fold of the freezer paper should face the center of the quilt and the edges of the freezer paper should slightly overlap the raw edges of the quilt. Secure the freezer paper to the quilt with straight pins.

5. With a ruler or flexible curve, extend, complete, or continue the pattern of your quilt, drawing it in pencil on the freezer paper. Be very precise with your markings, especially at the fold, in order for binding template to match up exactly with the quilt.

6. Make notes on the freezer paper as you design regarding color preferences or continuity, directional flow, and so on. Mark small arrows that indicate turned-under seam allowances. Pencil in the word *front* on this section of the freezer paper to remind yourself which side of the paper is the working side during the construction of the fabric binding.

7. Remove the freezer paper from the quilt. Set the quilt aside. Open the freezer paper. With a ruler or flexible curve, extend the lines of the pattern across the fold to the other half of the freezer-paper binding template. These markings make each template complete. Begin at the top of the binding strip and work

Step 4. Fold the freezer paper in half and place the fold against the binding line.

Step 5. Use a ruler or flexible curve to extend the quilt pattern onto the freezer paper.

Step 7. Unfold the freezer paper and extend the lines of the pattern.

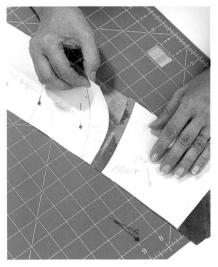

Step 9. No seam allowances are needed on the top or bottom edges, only between the templates. Pin prepared template to the waxed paper.

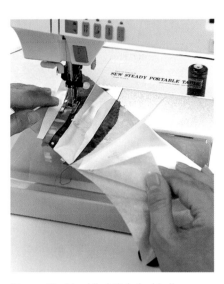

Step 10. Machine-blindstitch the binding templates to waxed paper.

Step 11. Fuse a lining strip inside the binding to keep dark fabrics from showing through lighter fabrics on the surface.

Step 12. Fold the fabric binding in half, then match up the fold to the binding line of the quilt top, making adjustments until pattern lines coincide.

downward, marking each line with little arrows that indicate the seam allowance to be turned under.

8. To ensure precision and stability during construction, use a rotary cutter and mat to cut out a strip of waxed paper to the same width and length as the freezer-paper binding template. The waxed paper acts as a stabilizer substitute. Its edges help you align the top and bottom edges of freezer-paper and fabric templates evenly and prevents distortion during piecing. The sewing machine needle perforates the waxed paper while you are stitching, and the waxed paper is easily torn away and discarded. Securely pin freezer paper shiny side down on top of the waxed paper. Do not cut the waxed paper during template construction.

9. Prepare each freezer-paper template as described in Chapter 1. Leave seam allowances along all curved seams of the templates but not on straight outer edges. Remember that the position of the turned-under seam is critical at the freezer-paper fold where it matches the corresponding seam in the quilt. Be sure it is as accurate as possible at that point. As you prepare each fabric template, keep the freezer paper in place and pin the entire template back in place on the waxed paper.

10. Machine-blindstitch the prepared fabric binding templates to each other, peeling back the freezer paper just enough to expose the seams. After you sew the entire strip of binding, remove the waxed paper by carefully tearing it away from the stitches. Remove the freezer paper. Trim the seams and edges.

11. Fold the fabric binding in half lengthwise, wrong sides together, and press. If you have light and dark values in your binding, you may have some shadowing where dark fabrics or seams show through the lighter colors. You can use white fabric as a lining in these problem areas to reduce transparency of lighter colors (see page 65).

12. Place the fold of the binding on the marked binding line of the quilt. Adjust the binding to the quilt so that the extended pattern on the binding matches the pattern on the quilt. Securely pin the binding to the quilt so there is no stretching, placing pins about 1″ (2.5 cm) apart. Machine-blindstitch the binding to the surface of the quilt. Press flat.

13. Once both left and right side bindings are in place, remeasure for the top and bottom bindings. Measure from side to side including attached side bindings. Add at least 2″ (5 cm) in case of error. Repeat Steps 3 through 12 to construct remaining binding strips.

14. After the binding is completed on all four sides, turn the quilt over. Fold the binding over to the back, turn under the raw edges, and whipstitch the binding to the quilt back.

Extending the Pattern into Curved Bindings

With a few changes and a bit more patience, you can use this same technique for binding quilts with curved edges. The beautiful effect is well worth the time and trouble!

The difference is that because the quilt's edges are curved, the freezer-paper binding strips will not fit flush against the sides for easy marking. You must measure the spaces between the quilt templates exactly and then transfer the measurements to a straight freezer-paper strip (doubled lengthwise as above).

Resting Place *detail. See full quilt on page 46.*

1. After you mark the curved binding line on the quilt, measure the space between each of the template lines on the quilt very carefully with a flexible curve that has a built-in ruler. Make sure the edge of the flexible curve conforms to and lies exactly on top of the marked binding line. Then measure and mark the amount of space on the center crease of the freezer-paper strip with a rigid metal or plastic ruler. Check for accuracy with your measurements and between the ruler and flexible curve.

2. From the pinpoint just marked, continue the flow of the template line as in Step 5 on page 64. It is important to cut all fabric templates on the bias to accommodate the curved edges.

3. For curved quilts, it's preferable to bind in one continuous motion. The best way is to make and stitch down the templates a section at a time as you work your way around the quilt. Start on the bottom right side. Piece about 3 or 4 feet, stitch the fabric templates together, remove the freezer paper on that section only, and fold and sew the binding to the quilt, leaving enough elbowroom for you to easily continue piecing the next section of templates. Use drafting tape to attach additional freezer-paper strips as needed.

4. Place the fold of the binding on the marked binding line of the quilt and adjust it so that the extended pattern on the binding matches the pattern and template seams on the quilt. Pin the binding seam to the quilt seam and conform the fold of the binding to match the curved borderline of the quilt edge. Adjust the fabric as necessary. Sew using the blindstitch. Fold the binding over to the back, turn under the raw edges, and whipstitch the binding to the quilt back.

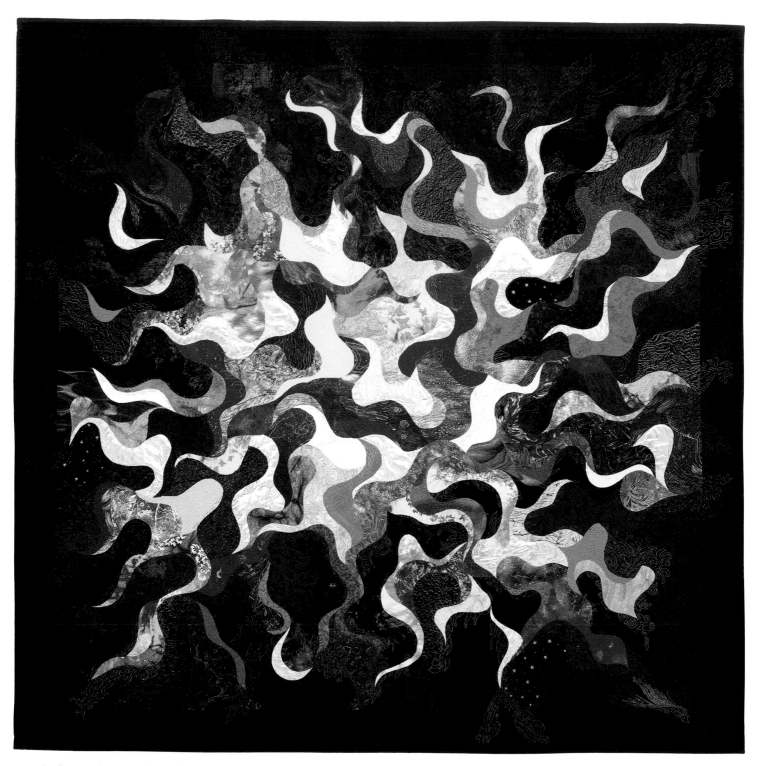

Portrait of My Soul, 1996, 65" × 65" (165 cm × 165 cm), cotton and lamé.

The idea for this quilt was conceived during a church service. As my mind wandered, I clearly visualized an image that I feel symbolizes my spirit. I see my spirit as a sunburst of energy, twisting and constantly moving, almost flickering. The vivid, colorful, flamelike shapes depict the emotions that affect me. Red symbolizes love and passion; purple, spirituality and sorrow; blue, happiness; yellow, joy; gray, fear and anxiety; and so forth. The gold lamé represents God. The black surrounding my spirit symbolizes the world. I completed the quilt exactly how I visualized it that evening in church.

CHAPTER 5

Free-Motion Stitching

*T*he opportunity to express your creativity as a quilter does not end with the completion of the pieced quilt top. The quilting stitches do not just hold the layers together but influence the overall look and feel of the quilt. Though I have seen incredibly beautiful hand-quilted pieces at shows and in magazines, I know that I lack the time, motivation, and patience to master the art of hand-work. Neither is traditional machine quilting right for me because I prefer curves to straight lines. I have found that for my quilts there is no better or more enjoyable way to sew the layers together than stitching freehand on the machine.

With free-motion stitching, I use thread to create new shapes and motifs that mimic the printed fabric pattern or complement the quilt top pattern. This adds a level of excitement to my quilts that I have been unable to achieve with traditional straight-line quilting methods. I also stitch with a variety of colorful threads—often using several strands at the same time to highlight or to soften particular sections of the pattern. Often intriguing, always spontaneous, once you get the hang of free-motion stitching, there is no more rewarding way to complete a quilt.

What Is Free-Motion Stitching?

Free-motion stitching is like using the sewing machine needle as a creative tool to quilt random, impromptu designs in thread. Traditional straight-line quilting requires a standard walking foot attachment. The machine's feed dogs, which guide the needle, remain fixed in place. The major difference is that with free-motion stitching the *feed dogs* are lowered. Also, you use a darning foot in place of the walking foot attachment. Lowering the feed dogs allows you to move the quilt through the machine in almost any way you choose. The needle remains stationary, and you move the quilt in order to create patterns. Stitching curved lines is effortless, and it is easy to switch directions. You can stitch up and down, side to side, or in circles. There is no need to prepare stencils or to draw lines onto the fabric. You are free to create or modify the quilting design as you sew. You can echo the patterns in the quilt top, or you can create entirely new motifs. You can even doodle, just as you would on a sketch pad!

Creating a Workspace

As for any machine quilting, for free-motion stitching you will need a well-lit, uncluttered workspace around your sewing machine that will support the weight and bulk of the quilt or project you are working on. You cannot move the quilt around freely and produce quality stitching if your work area is cluttered up with fabrics, notions, or other items. Clear it all away before you start stitching.

It is important to adjust all surrounding work surfaces so they are level with the machine needle plate. A level sewing surface enables you to slide a bulky quilt around freely with minimum physical effort and a minimum of stitch distortion and drag on the needle during the quilting process. There are commercial cabinets for sewing machines that feature a multilevel shelf. You can adjust the shelf so that it holds the machine at the correct height for a level workspace. These cabinets are available at some sewing machine dealers and through mail order. It's just as easy to rig your own level work surface by using several rectangular tables adjusted to the same height as the sewing machine needle plate.

Setting Up the Machine

For most machines, setting up for free-motion stitching simply involves lowering the feed dogs and attaching a darning foot. Some machines also require a special throat plate to cover the feed dogs. Check your instruction manual or consult your dealer before you begin. Here's how to get started.

1. Lower the machine feed dogs or install a throat plate to cover them. This allows you to stitch in any direction you please— up and down, side to side, or in circles—while the quilt stays in the same position in front of you.

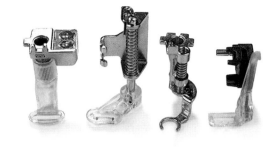

2. Adjust the top tension so that the stitch joins somewhere in the middle of the quilt sandwich. If the bobbin thread comes to the surface, lower the top tension. If the top thread is loose, loops, or is prominent on the back surface, tighten the top tension.

3. Set the machine on a regular straight stitch.

4. Attach a darning foot. I always prefer an open-toe foot, which makes it easier to see the stitches.

5. For learning purposes, thread the machine with regular-weight sewing thread. Thread it so that the spool unwinds to the machine from a vertical (upright) reel and the thread unwinds from the back of the spool, not from the front.

Shown here are darning feet for various machines. The third one is an open-toe darning foot

6. Use a snug tension in the bobbin. Check to see if your dealer recommends that you purchase a spare bobbin case for this type of stitching. This may save time and frustration in making regular adjustments.

7. Replace the regular machine needle with a 90/14 topstitch needle. I have found this needle, with its elongated eye, works best, especially when using multiple strands of thread. I have used a 90 jeans/denim needle in a pinch or with a single strand of thread, but I prefer the topstitch needle because the eye is so much bigger.

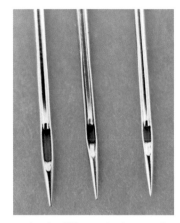

Notice the difference in the eyes of the needles. On the left is a top-stitch needle with an elongated eye; in the middle is a jeans needle; on the right is a standard machine needle.

Ready to Stitch

When learning free-motion stitching, your primary goal should be to make stitches that are uniform in length. Aim for a constant and consistent momentum both with quilt movement and machine speed. If you move the quilt through the machine too fast or the machine speed is too slow, the stitches will be long. If you move the quilt through too slow or the machine speed is too fast, the stitches will be tiny. Running the machine at an inconsistent speed results in jerky, uneven lines and thread breakage, especially with temperamental metallic threads. Learning to move the fabric smoothly and at a consistent speed is the most important thing you can practice. Follow the steps here to practice with a sample.

1. Prepare a sample quilt sandwich, about 20″ × 20″ (50 cm × 50 cm), using muslin or old fabrics. Layer it just as you would a quilt, with a surface fabric, one or two pieces of stabilizer, batting, and backing fabric. The extra weight of the stabilizer secures and improves the stitch tension. Use safety pins to secure the layers, or, if you prefer, baste them together to keep them from shifting.

2. Place the prepared sandwich under the needle. Start free-motion stitching in the center of the quilt sandwich. Use the handwheel of your sewing machine to lower the needle into the throat plate and pick up the bobbin thread. Bring up the bobbin thread to the surface of the sandwich and, together with the top thread, hold them to the back and left of and beneath the darning foot. It's

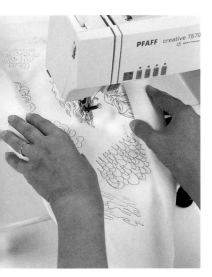

Step 5. Hold the project loosely on both sides, jelly-roll fashion. Relax your body, especially your hands, to avoid cramping as you stitch.

important to bring the bobbin thread to the surface each time you begin stitching to ensure a smooth start for the quilting process. It prevents the thread from tangling, jamming, or matting on the backside of the sandwich.

3. Lower the sewing foot lifter (lever) to the appropriate darning position for your machine. This creates the tension for your stitches. It is important to remember this step, yet it's so easy to forget! If you don't lower the sewing foot lifter, you'll end up with a tangled mess of thread on the backside of the quilt— it's not a pretty sight and you'll have to rip it all out!

4. While still holding the thread, take one tiny stitch forward, one stitch back, and another stitch forward to lock the stitch in place. Remember: now your feed dogs are down, so you must manually move the sandwich back and forth to do these stitches. Snip off the excess thread tails close to the surface.

5. Loosely roll the right and left sides of the quilt sandwich toward the needle, leaving a span of 6″ (15 cm) or so of unrolled fabric surface area around and under the needle. Gently grasp the rolled surface in your hands.

6. Slowly put pressure on the foot pedal and begin the stitching. Move the sandwich around for a few minutes to familiarize yourself with this type of quilting and to become comfortable with the feeling of freedom and creativity at your fingertips. Keep an eye out for the safety pins that are holding the layers together. Remove them before you begin stitching in an area and don't allow the darning foot to get hung up on them.

7. There are two variables in free-motion stitching: the speed of the machine and the speed with which you move the fabric. Experiment to find out what happens to the stitches at different machine speeds. Practice moving around the fabric sandwich at different rates of speed. To stop the stitching process, take a couple of tiny stitches back and forth, as you did when you started. Snip the thread close to the surface.

When you begin this type of stitching, your natural tendency is to run the machine at a very slow speed. As you progress and gain confidence, your pace will increase. Actually, you maintain better control and will have smoother, more even stitches using a little faster speed than a slow one.

8. Once you become accustomed to the idea of creating your own stitches, try to doodle with the needle. Try some loop-'d-loops, figure eights, hearts, teardrops, triangles, circles, or zigzags. Try writing your name. Draw a flower and then a leaf. Have fun and don't be concerned about what your stitches look like. It doesn't matter how uneven or how jerky they are. You are learning, and like all things in life, your stitching will improve with time and practice. Continue free-motion stitching for as long as you please to gain confidence.

Echoing a Motif in Fabric

To echo a motif in fabric, make another quilt sandwich, except this time use fabric for the top surface that has an open, flowing, unsymmetrical, large-scaled print. Echo the print, stitching freely around it. Don't try to stitch directly on the lines. Instead, loosely follow them as a guide. Exaggerate the print. Mimic it. Reinvent it. Play outside the lines! Try to add your own creative touch to the print.

Try echoing the fabric's print and then mimic stitching in other areas of the quilt.

Mayhem in My Garden *detail. See the full quilt on page 106.*

Freehand Stitching

Freehand stitching is quilting without a design on the fabric to follow. To practice freehand stitching, make a third quilt sandwich, with solid surface fabric this time. Now try to stitch freehand the echo quilting design you just practiced. It doesn't matter that you think you can't draw; try it anyway. Freehand-stitch a daisy or other flower with a center and all the petals. Draw your version of leaves, butterflies, flames, water, a bird, a fish, the sun, a cloud, a balloon—anything you can think of. Have fun with this!

Using Multiple Threads in Your Quilts

I quilt most of my works with two strands of thread. I've successfully used three and even up to four strands of thread through a single needle on some quilts. Why? For the same reason I use so many different fabrics in my quilts! It adds interest and excitement, depth and texture. And it's so much fun to work with the all the different color combinations!

Also, I've found that when sewing with metallic ribbon threads, such as Sulky Sliver, I have better luck keeping the threads from snapping when I use two strands of thread together, rather than a single strand. The second strand seems to give added strength to the first one.

For your first attempt at using multiple threads for quilting, I suggest that you use 40 wt. decorative rayon threads rather than metallic threads. Thread breakage is seldom a problem with multiple rayon threads, and they give you fewer tension problems—both with the machine and for you! You'll need a vertical thread spool holder that accommodates two spools of thread and a top-stitch needle with a large eye.

Free-Motion Designs

The sixteen designs on this and the following pages were all made using free-motion stitching. To help you practice a variety of shapes, each is accompanied by a sketch that shows the direction of the stitching. To try out one of these designs, just follow the arrows. The numbers are there to help make sure you don't get lost!

Curls 'n' Crescents

Leaves

Fantasy Vine

Shells

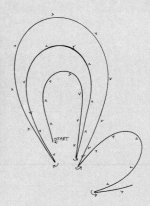

Dogwood

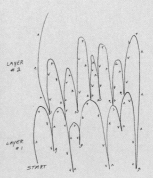

Angel Wings

Seaweed

Vikki's Fire

Aflame

Water

Crabapple Blossoms

Geometrics

Free-Motion Designs (continued)

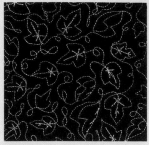

Ivy

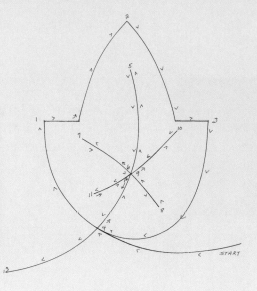

Tail Feathers

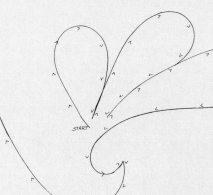

Fiddleheads

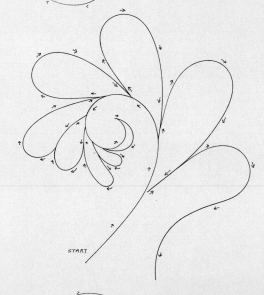

Curlicue

Thread Combinations

Until you are familiar with quilting with multiple threads, I recommend that you use only combinations of the same types of thread. Use all rayon or all flat metallic threads, for example. For learning purposes, the stitching is smoother and less problematic when the threads are the same.

After you become comfortable with using two threads in your quilting, you may wish to look at the possibilities of using all different combinations of thread: rayon/twisted metallic, acrylic/Sulky Sliver metallic, rayon/Sulky Sliver metallic, and so on. Mixing together different types of thread provides some unusual and exciting results.

Threading the Machine

Amazing effects are made possible by adding a second thread that brings extra color into your free-motion stitches. Make sure that both threads unwind from an upright (vertical), not horizontal, position.

If your machine isn't equipped with two vertical thread reels, check with your dealer to see what accessories are available. There are some commercial thread holders available in stores and by mail order that accommodate multiple spools of thread for decorative stitching. However, I suggest you first try the free-motion technique for a while and then decide whether or not you like it before spending the money. In the meantime, it's quite easy to rig up a makeshift multiple-thread system (see page 78).

If you are using two threads of the same type (for example, two rayon or two metallic Sulky Sliver threads), you may thread the machine and needle with both threads, holding them together, smoothly and as one. Usually, you get good results with this method of threading the machine when combining threads of the same type. You must flatten the threads together, maintaining the smoothness

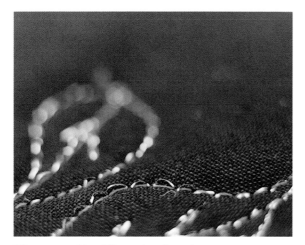

When you combine different threads, such as rayon or metallics, one of them may loop up from the line.

Here, the same stitching design is done correctly. Threads should lie flat.

A Little Ingenuity with Thread Holders

Though hundreds of new sewing accessories come on the market each year, it sometimes seems I can never find exactly what I'm looking for. It either is unavailable or costs more than I want to pay, so I rig up my workspace to suit my own purpose.

It's not fancy, but this is how I set up my machine for sewing with multiple threads. I found an old-fashioned wooden thread holder that is meant to be hung on the wall. I sawed off a section of the holder that contains a row of thread reels. I lay this on its side next to the sewing machine so the wooden reels are slanted up and away from the machine.

I also found an inexpensive cone thread holder at a local fabric store, one that comes with a tall metal hook. I tape the metal hook onto the back right corner of my machine, making sure the tape doesn't interfere with any moving parts. I remove the tape promptly after stitching to avoid leaving tape residue on my machine. You may also keep the metal hook in its original holder if you prefer and weigh down the base of the cone holder to keep it from moving. Put the threads through the loop in the metal hook before threading your machine. The hook stands taller than the machine, and the strands of thread reach upward and away from the reels as the thread feeds into the machine. This keeps the flow of thread smooth and untangled. Some unruly threads insist on freely unwinding in ringlets from their spools and wrapping around the reels, causing a problem. Using the tall metal hook as a thread guide helps solve that problem by holding the thread steady and in place in an upward position.

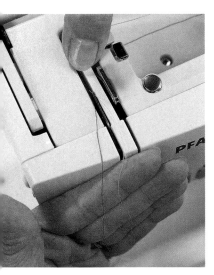

To prevent looping, thread each strand separately into the threading slot—one on the right and one on the on the left of the metal divider, or tension disk.

between your fingers to get out any bends or kinks. This is especially important with the ribbonlike metallics.

If you are using two threads, whether of the same type or a combination, and have a problem with the thread not lying flat on the surface (looping), the problem may be solved by using a different method of threading your sewing machine.

As you thread the machine, you must put the thread through two threading slots on the front of the machine. The first threading slot, on the left, has what appears to be a metal divider, called a *thread tension disk*. The thread tension disk regulates the top thread tension on your machine. Normally you may guide the thread to either the left or to the right of the thread tension disk when you are threading your machine. If you cannot find the thread tension disk on your machine, consult your dealer for help.

Put one of the threads to the right of the thread tension disk and the other thread to the left. Then continue to thread the machine normally. This procedure alone may alleviate some of the thread looping problem. If you still are not satisfied with the appearance of the thread, you may have to adjust the top tension dial a bit more. It is the nature of some metallic threads to arc. Don't fret so much over the small or tiny loops. It is the large and very noticeable loops you want to avoid.

If you are using three or four threads, divide the threads between the two sides of the metal tension disk, one or two threads to each side, the left and the right. Keep the same types of threads together.

Thread both strands of thread through the needle's eye. If you have a sewing machine with a built-in needle threader, you are fortunate indeed. This is an amenity that's easy on the eyes, and a godsend for quilting with several threads. If you are ever in the market for a new sewing machine, this is definitely an option you'll want to consider. Otherwise, handheld needle threaders are available in the notions department of the fabric store.

I can't stress enough the importance of keeping the threads, especially metallic ribbon threads, flat and smooth during the stitching process. If you see the thread is not flowing evenly and is kinky or twisted, stop, smooth the thread out with your fingers, and rethread the machine.

Changing Threads

To change threads, guide your needle to a seam in the surface of your project and tie off the threads by taking tiny stitches back and forth.

1. If you are stitching with two or multiple threads and you want to change a single thread color without tying off the others, stop the machine with the needle down.
2. Snip the thread you want to change, leaving about a 5-inch (12.5 cm) tail from the needle.
3. Raise the sewing foot lifter to release the tension and remove the thread spool from the reel.
4. Replace with the new color of thread and rethread the machine.
5. Lower the sewing foot lifter.
6. When you move the handwheel to thread the take-up lever, the needle will move to an upright position. Be very careful not to shift or move the quilt project, as you want the bobbin thread to remain stationary.
7. Remove the old color from the needle's eye, leaving the other strand intact.
8. Rethread the needle with the new thread.
9. Hold the 5-inch (12.5 cm) tail of the old color and the new strand together and to the left and rear of the needle.
10. Take tiny stitches back and forth, snip the tails at the surface, and continue stitching.

Varying Bobbin Color

You have several choices regarding bobbin thread color. You may use the same color thread in the bobbin that you are using on the surface of the quilt. This eliminates some tension adjustment difficulties, because if the bobbin thread does happen to come to the quilt surface, it won't be as noticeable. The drawback is that if you change surface thread color often, you need to change the bobbin color as well.

Because I use multiple threads, change colors constantly, and frequently design back art for my quilts, my concern is to choose a bobbin thread color that blends in best with the fabric and pattern on the quilt back. Often it is a medium to medium-dark value gray, or any color that matches or blends with the predominate background fabric color for both the quilt back and front surface.

You may choose to utilize different-colored threads or types of decorative thread for the bobbin that will add to the design and texture to the backside

Looping Tip

If you are using multiple threads and a single thread bows or loops and absolutely nothing you do helps the cause, use the tip of your extra long tweezers or seam ripper to reach underneath the biggest loop and gently tug at it in an upward motion. This makes the loop even bigger as it tightens the surrounding stitches. Then snip off each end of the loop at the surface. The other strand of thread holds the remaining stitching in place.

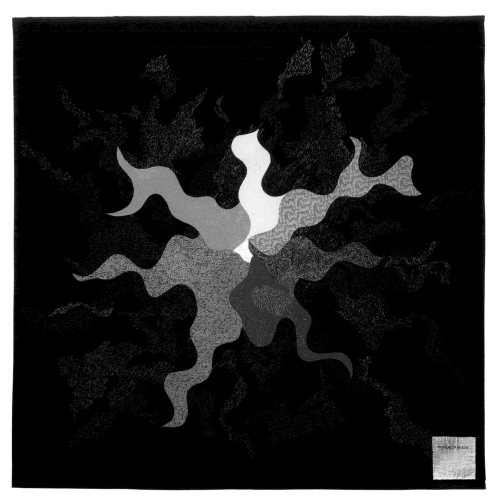

Circle of Emotions, 1996, 65″ × 65″ (165 cm × 165 cm).
Back art of Portrait of My Soul. *See the front of the quilt on page 68. I used different colors of rayon thread in the bobbin to achieve the effect of flames on the quilt backing. The rest of the bobbin thread was regular-weight polyester that matched the background color.*

of your quilt, especially if you do backing art. If you do use rayon or metallic threads in the bobbin, you may need to loosen the bobbin tension a bit to prevent thread breakage. Keep in mind that using rayon or metallic in the bobbin can be done, but it is tricky and will take added patience and effort on your part. I don't recommend doing this until you are very comfortable with this type of stitching.

More About Top and Bobbin Tensions

Continually adjusting the sewing machine's top tension during stitching and after changing threads is a habit you will need to get into when doing free-motion stitching. There is no one perfect setting. The best tension settings for multiple threads, type of thread, and even sometimes colors of thread vary. Most often, it simply involves a minor adjustment—a hair in either direction. This is a trial-and-error proposition, and sometimes you have to play around awhile to get it just right.

Tips for Beautiful Free-Motion Stitching

- Don't take on too much too soon. First try your hand with a practice sandwich, as described on pages 71–72. Move on to a pillow cover or similar small projects to perfect the technique before you start on your first pieced quilt top.

- When you begin each day of free-motion stitching on your quilt, take about ten minutes to warm up on a prepared practice quilt sandwich first. It takes a few minutes to relax, get into the spirit, and recapture the old rhythm of stitching again.

- For a look of continuity, begin and end your free-motion stitching in a seam whenever possible.

- Start stitching as close to the center of the project as you can and work equally on all sides toward the outside edges. Working from the center out in all directions helps keep any distortion or stretch in the surface fabric under control, flat and smooth. Otherwise, you may find yourself literally trapped in a corner, between two completed areas of stitching, and will have to ease in all the fullness from excess surface fabric.

- Look where you're going! Try not to focus on the needle while you are stitching—you need to see what is happening to the stitch design all around you. If you don't, you're likely to run over your own stitches or leave gaps in the design. As you stitch, keep one eye on the needle, but keep the other eye on the open road of fabric ahead.

- Think one step ahead. As you stitch, keep in mind what direction you want to go next and find the best way to get where you want to be. Continually maintaining a good needle "takeoff position" as you do free-motion stitching is necessary for a smooth quilting effect. Always try to maneuver the needle toward the empty areas where you want to stitch the next motif. Use *Curlicue*, *Water*, or *Curls 'n' Crescents* curved free-motion stitches as needed to set up your needle to a good takeoff position for the next motif.

- When switching thread types and combinations, test for any tension problems on a test quilt sandwich first rather than your quilt. This will save you from a lot of time spent ripping out stitches!

- If you know in advance that you are going to quilt your project heavily with three or four strands of thread, either use a medium-weight stabilizer during construction, or add another layer of lightweight stabilizer to the quilt sandwich to give added strength to your stitches.

- While stitching, consider playing soft, restful background music with a consistent tempo. Not only does music relax you as you work, but it will help you maintain a rhythm.

Ideally, the top and bobbin tensions should be adjusted so the top and bobbin threads adjoin and embed in the middle of the quilt sandwich. Trying to achieve this perfection will tax your patience and good humor. If the bobbin tension is too loose, the bobbin thread will show on the top surface of the quilt. There may be times when for creative purposes, this is what you want, to add a splash of bobbin color to the surface. Most times, however, this is undesirable. If the perfect tension combination is eluding you for the moment, it is better to err the other way, and have the top threads barely peek through the backside of the quilt.

Tension settings differ among brands and types of sewing machines, too. Check your owner's manual or with your sewing machine dealer for information on how to loosen and tighten both the top and bobbin tensions for your particular machine.

With free-motion stitching, I've found that keeping a snug bobbin tension usually works the best, especially when using multiple threads through the same needle. A snug tension helps pull the bulky surface threads beneath the surface.

Relieving Tension—Yours!

One key to mastering free-motion stitching is to relax. If you are tense or nervous, your shoulders will hunch and your fingers will tighten. Instead of smooth, flowing lines, you'll end up with jerky, uneven stitches—and sore muscles!

Use a good chair for support, and adjust it until you find a comfortable height in relation to the sewing machine. Make sure you have good light; you want to see exactly how your work is turning out. Before you take the first stitch, take a moment to compose your thoughts. Begin with a general idea of how you want the stitching to look. Then relax and let the stitches flow. Remain flexible and open to new design ideas. If you stay overly loyal to your original thoughts, you will become tense because the stitching doesn't look the way you envisioned, and your work (and creativity) will suffer.

If, however, you experience a pulling sensation while stitching the project, the bobbin tension may be too tight and need loosening. Normally, I use regular-weight polyester thread in the bobbin spool.

Troubleshooting

Working with specialty threads, especially metallics, is tricky on the best of days. Some days the threads flow beautifully, you do beautiful work, and you get a lot accomplished. The next day the very same threads can be finicky, fickle, and downright obstinate.

If your thread is breaking or is not flowing freely, the following tips may help.

• Try a new needle. Change needles often when doing free-motion stitching. Sometimes I change needles every few hours. The friction of the threads, especially metallic threads, wears the eye of the needle and causes the thread to break. Don't skimp on the needles; the cost is not worth your good humor!

• Always use a topstitch needle. The larger eye means less friction and is necessary for multiple thread usage. If you are using three or four threads and breakage is a problem, try using a 100 topstitch needle. It creates a larger hole in the fabric for the threads to pass through.

• Maintain a consistent sewing speed. Avoid jerky stops and starts that cause metallic threads to snap. Start slowly and build speed.

• Look for knots or kinks in the thread, particularly in a metallic thread, that would prevent it from flowing through the needle's eye smoothly.

• Sometimes the thread is flawed. If it gives you trouble consistently, throw it out. Also, thread from almost-empty spools may present problems. You are not saving money by trying to use up old thread—it can give you headaches and heartaches. Discard it.

• If the top thread mats or loops on the backside, check to make sure the machine is threaded correctly on top.

• Is your top or bobbin tension too tight? Try a lower tension (see pages 80–82).

• Is the needle hole in the throat plate smooth? File down any metal snags on the throat plate with a nail file.

• Check that thread is wrapped properly onto its spool, not tangled or knotted.

• Threads should unwind from vertical thread spools as you sew. Unwinding vertically prevents the threads, especially metallics, from twisting.

• Threads will snap if they get tangled in or wrapped around the thread spool reels. This happens when the plastic thread spool continues to spin after the machine has stopped stitching. Cut out a little donut-shaped pad from a piece of felt and fit it onto the bottom of the thread reel to prevent the thread spool from spinning.

• Either remove or punch an adequately sized hole in the paper labels attached to the ends of the thread spool. The glue on labels can stick to the thread reel and prevent the spool from spinning freely.

• Make sure there are no renegade threads or debris caught up in the threading slots or tension disks of your machine. You'll need a flashlight to peek inside the opening. Unplug the machine and remove broken threads with the extra long tweezers or see your dealer for help.

• Are your bobbin case and bobbin clean? If you are using a plastic bobbin, is it warped or chipped? Unless your machine is prelubricated, put a couple of drops of good grade sewing machine oil on a cotton swab and thoroughly clean the inside of the bobbin case. Sticky debris builds up inside the case and on the bobbin, causing uneven spin. Check with your dealer regarding oiling your machine. Some are prelubricated and do not need oiling; others should be oiled after every eight to ten hours of free-motion stitching.

Portrait of My Soul *detail. See the full quilt on page 68.*

• Is the thread wound smoothly and evenly on the bobbin?

• Remove the needleplate and clean debris from underneath it and from the feed dogs. Use a stiff artist's paintbrush to sweep out the sewing hook area and a cotton swab with a drop of oil to clean off the dirt.

• Brush away lint from the bobbin area often. Debris really accumulates fast with free-motion stitching.

• If a strand of thread snaps while you are stitching, stop immediately, retrieve the thread tail, and rethread the machine. You don't want the thread to get tangled inside the tension disks.

Practice and Patience

One of the joys of free-motion stitching is that the design comes together quickly, with almost immediate results. This is also one of the reasons why free-motion stitching requires practice and patience. The machine does move fast, and often you need to make split-second decisions.

If you make a mistake and the design is not working out exactly how you planned, stop to reconsider before you reach for your seam ripper. Ripping out the stitches is time-consuming and difficult. Each time you do it, you lose a little more patience and you risk damaging the fabrics in the quilt. I think it is better, especially for a beginner, to accept that there are some areas of stitching you are not totally satisfied with. As you practice and complete more quilts, your expertise will grow. Moreover, once the design is complete, tiny imperfections will be noticeable to no one but you. Instead of worrying about patches of poor stitching, use them as a learning experience. Move on, relax, and enjoy stitching the rest of the quilt.

It's said that patience is a virtue. Remember, works of art don't come fast or easy! Enjoy the creative process for what it is. Keep at it, don't give up, and you will have a beautiful quilt to show for your effort!

Creation of the Sun and Stars, 1998, 65″ × 75″ (165 cm × 190 cm).

God's omnipotence, symbolized by the yellow ribbons, flows from all corners of the heavens to form our sun, the cranberry orb. As the newly born sun spins, fire and flames are thrown back into the universe, eventually transforming into joyful, dancing stars.

Striking Out on Your Own

By now, you are familiar with the topstitch piecing technique and may have tried some of the quilt top patterns in Chapter 2. This chapter takes you through the steps of designing your own quilt top, from inspiration to sketch to numbered templates. You'll even learn about improvisational quilts, which you design as your piece.

Even if you have made several traditional quilts before, the prospect of designing an original quilt top for which no pattern is provided is both exciting and a little nerve-racking. My advice is to remember that you have all the skills you need to do this. If you believe in yourself, are persistent, and put your heart into your work, you can design your own quilt tops. And you will discover that there are few experiences that bring as much pride and joy as completing a quilt that you have designed yourself.

Conceiving of a New Quilt Top

Your quilt is the place where you share happiness and sorrows, zeal and frustrations, love and loss. With every fabric you choose and every stitch that you make, you are conveying those feelings to others who see your work. This is why the search for ideas for a new quilt top pattern is so personal. The quilt is about you and your perspective on life, and so there is no magic formula that will give you the inspiration you need. I feel that the inspirations that appear in everyday life are special gifts and cannot be brought forth on demand. However, you may be more receptive to ideas and inspirations when you are relaxed and open-minded. When you are searching for an idea for a new quilt, I suggest you follow these six guidelines. They will help you to relax, free your imagination, and allow the ideas to flow.

• Learn to be patient with yourself. If you are able to achieve a peaceful state of mind, you are more likely to be in touch with your feelings and more able to translate them to your quilt. Take the time each day to relax and nurture your senses. Look at the world around you and explore it as if you were a child seeing it for the first time. For some, listening to music helps soothe the mind; for others, lighting aromatic candles or incense calms the spirit. Create a serene environment around yourself and allow yourself the freedom to daydream.

• Keep an open mind. Finding creative inspiration is much easier if you are flexible. Be willing to look at life from different perspectives. For example, when thinking of colors, do not limit yourself to choosing shades of blue for the sky or shades of green for the grass. It is the unexpected that surprises and delights us when we look at a quilt. What if the grass were orange or the sky purple? What would those color choices say about your perspective on life?

• Consider what it is about you, your experiences, and your outlook on life that is unique. Your original way of looking at a subject can speak to others and touch them in ways you could never imagine. We are all different, and it is our differences that most directly influence our art. Once you are aware of your own uniqueness, have the courage to express it. If you learn to believe in yourself and trust your feelings, you will please the only person whose opinion of your work really matters—you.

• Devote time to the creative process. Action begets creativity. I believe that we quilt not only to relax, but also to nurture the soul. Decide how much time you are able to give to your quilting and schedule your day so that you are able to work with energy and without interruption. Self-discipline is difficult, but the rewards are many. You will find that once you are able to establish a routine, your enthusiasm builds, and the momentum of each day's successes carries you forward.

• Learn from mistakes. Fear of failure keeps too many talented people from discovering the joy of designing their own quilts. Yet making mistakes is a necessary part of learning any new skill. Never strive for perfection. Instead, look at your mistakes as an opportunity to grow creatively. A lot of my work is the result of mistakes I made, for which I needed inventive solutions to fix.

- Be passionate, because passion is the most important freedom of all. Please don't be afraid to put your entire heart and soul into your work. The only way to develop a style that is original and authentic is to work from your very being within and let your passion flow out. Releasing the emotions and ideas within you is not only mentally and spiritually fulfilling but also healing; it brings the most satisfying and joyful feeling of accomplishment. Work created with your passion and enthusiasm is special. It is who you are. When you share yourself in your work it is clearly visible to others and you will convey your emotions to influence all who see it.

Looking for Ideas in All the Right Places

You can never tell where the idea for your next quilt is going to come from. Some ideas hit you from out of the blue; others take their good sweet time and develop over the years. Inspirations are seldom convenient. The trick is to be prepared. Even if you are not confident of your drawing abilities, it pays to keep a sketch pad close at hand. A vivid inspiration for *Creation of the Sun and Stars* came to me at 5:30 A.M. on a morning I'd planned to sleep in. The idea was beautiful; the timing was not! I roused myself enough to sketch a rough draft on a notepad I keep on my nightstand.

Ideas can fade as quickly as they come. If you take the time to write down the concept or make a sketch on paper, you have a better chance of remembering details and why the image appealed to you. Use your sketch pad to jot down possible colors, too, and to organize your thoughts. Draw simple outlines and shapes. Later, when you are ready to start a new quilt, you can look back through the pages of your sketch pad and decide which ideas have potential.

Begin a collection of images that appeal to you. Look at books, postcards, newspapers, magazines, flower catalogs, and even junk mail. Decide which color combinations and shapes please you and look for similar images. Keep all your clippings in one place so you can find them!

I look for abstract photos that feature curved lines and shapes and also collect detailed images that I think I might use in the future as a reference when drawing a design. Few people can draw the exact shape and detail of a flower or know the shape of a lightning bolt without referring to a picture. I have an ever-growing collection of images like these, and I go through them whenever I am looking for a reference guide or new starting point. I used a picture from a piece of junk mail as a reference for the lightning bolts on the backside of *Breaking Point*.

Making Simple Sketches

If you are designing your first original quilt top, my advice is to keep it small and keep it simple. Too many times, I've seen talented and enthusiastic beginners tackle projects that are too big or too complex. They quickly become frustrated and lose heart. Once you have gained confidence and practiced your skills on smaller pieces, there will be time to make the quilt you have dreamed of. To

Inspiration from Nature

Like many quilters, I look to nature for inspiration for my quilts. I've found the best way to study the world around me is to use my camera. Take snapshots of scenes that move you. Take shots from different perspectives and at different times of day. When you are ready to translate those photographic images into fabric, feel free to take artistic license. You do not need to re-create the scene exactly as the camera captured it. Leave perfection and detail to the camera—it is your impressions of a scene that are important for your quilt.

I am in love with the beauty in nature, and for me, it is a rich and endless source of inspiration for my quilting. Blacklick Pond, in a metro park close to me, influenced three of my quilt tops. I treasure the serenity and seclusion I find there. So far, I've made quilts to celebrate three of the four seasons on the pond.

Hanging out on the lily pad.

Feelin' Groovy, *back of* Blacklick Pond: Reflections at Twilight.

Water lilies are among my favorite flowers.

Blacklick Pond: Reflections at Twilight.

Fall leaves floating on Blacklick Pond.

Tears on Blacklick Pond *detail. See the full quilt on page xviii.*

Winter ice on Blacklick Pond.

Sand from a North Carolina beach was the inspiration for Angel Wings.

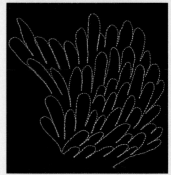

Free-motion stitching design, Angel Wings.

Fire and Ice *detail. See the full quilt on page 14.*

A beautiful dragonfly in summer.

Blacklick Pond: Reflections at Twilight *detail. See full quilt on page viii.*

Try a design made from simple curved lines.

begin, I recommend limiting the size to a 12″ to 15″ (30 cm to 36 cm) square. You can use the finished piece as a block in a larger quilt or as a pillow cover or small wall hanging. Keep the total number of templates down to eight or nine.

Whether you are using a photograph, a clipping, or memory for inspiration, begin by sketching that idea on paper. You will use these sketches as a basis for drawing up a full-sized pattern, or *master pattern*, and a set of templates. Don't let the blank sheet of paper sit in front of you for too long—pick up your pencil and draw. All you need as a starting point is a series of lines and shapes. There is no need for detail or even for color in this first sketch. Remember to keep the pattern simple—this will make the quilt much easier to construct when you are ready to cut fabric and start sewing.

Think About Mood

Before you begin to draw, give some thought to the mood that you wish to create in your quilt. What feelings or emotions do you wish it to convey to the people who view it? You can portray different moods in your pattern by using different types of lines. Curved lines, for example, have a calming and graceful effect. Vertical lines can give an illusion of height; horizontal lines can imply distance; diagonal lines suggest movement; and broken or jagged lines suggest discord. Lines and color together can make a strong statement. In *Fire and Ice* (see page 14), the uneven lines and cool colors of the icicles are in direct contrast to the graceful curves and powerful colors of the fire. My intent was to show passion in contrast with frigidity, movement opposite stillness.

Experiment with Shapes

If you have made traditional, geometric quilts before, you are already familiar with shapes that are symmetrical, like triangles, squares, and hexagons. Topstitch piecing appliqué allows you to add smooth, elegant curves to your repertoire. The asymmetry of these shapes will bring a quality of motion and grace to your quilt. As we have seen, the flexible curve is a very useful tool. Be sure to use it to experiment with curved lines. This simple tool gives you sensational curved patterns. Take time to play with it and experience the freedom it can give you in designing your own patterns. I have used the flexible curve on almost every one of my quilt patterns.

Sketch the Focal Point

Begin by deciding what image or theme you want to be the focal point, or major element of interest, in your pattern. A quilt can have a single focal point, as in the tree in *Breaking Point*, on page vii, or the spiral in *Fire Within*, on page 32. A quilt can also have more than one focal point that makes up its theme, such as the leaves in *Tears on Blacklick Pond*, on page xviii, or *Blacklick Pond: Reflections at Twilight*, on page viii. Look for interesting angles or perspectives from which to draw your focal point. Consider how, for example, a fish might look if seen from above instead of from below. In *Upstream* on page 91, for example, the focal point is drawn from an unusual perspective.

Upstream by Elizabeth Palmer-Spilker, 1998, 33" × 43" (84 cm × 109 cm).
In the collection of Alison Lauter. Here, the focal point is viewed from above.

Draw your focal point on your blank sheet of paper first and make it dominant. Avoid the temptation to draw it in the dead center of your paper. Your composition is likely to be more interesting if the focal point is off-center, both vertically and horizontally.

If you lack confidence in your drawing abilities, draw the focal point on a piece of scrap paper first. Once you are pleased with the way it looks, slip it under your drawing paper so that the lines show through. You can then simply trace it onto the master design. The same goes for other elements of the composition.

When creating *Blacklick Pond: Reflections at Twilight* (page viii), for example, I drew each of the lily pads and flowers separately on scraps of paper. I drew them in various sizes, and each was formed slightly different from the others. Once they were all drawn, I slid them beneath my master pattern and positioned them as I desired. If you have one, a light table is very useful—you will be able to see each sketch clearly beneath the master pattern. If you don't have a light table, just make sure you use a dark pencil to draw the sketches; the lines should show through. Rearrange the elements until you are pleased with the composition.

When your focal point is drawn, turn your attention to the background, or *negative space*, on the rest of the sketch (the focal point occupies *positive space*). The areas that make up the background in your sketch are just as important to the pattern's composition as the focal point. Keep in mind that whatever is happening in the background shouldn't overpower the focal point, but complement it. Add interest to the background composition by varying sizes and shapes.

Don't expect that the first sketch you make will be your final pattern. Each time you redraw the sketch, the pattern evolves. With every new pencil stroke, you are bringing in new ideas. Try not to limit yourself to the first lines or shapes you draw. Instead, allow yourself the freedom to let the pattern develop.

From Sketch to Master Pattern

When you have a sketch that pleases you, you're ready to create your full-scale master pattern that will serve as your blueprint when you are constructing your quilt. There are several ways to enlarge your sketch.

You can draw your pattern directly onto paper that is cut to the actual size you want the quilt to be. For creating the master pattern I use drawing paper that comes on a roll, available up to a width of 60″ (150 cm) from artist supply stores. For larger patterns, I simply tape two or more sheets together. For simple quilts and smaller projects such as pillow covers or single blocks, this method of getting your pattern to the correct size may be the best way to go.

To draw the master pattern directly on paper, begin by estimating the finished size and cutting or taping a sheet of paper to that size. Always add a little extra in case you decide to make changes as the quilt progresses and to accommodate borders and binding. Lay the paper on a table or other flat surface. The paper may tend to curl up after being on a roll; if so, secure its edges with tape. Use a sharp, dark-leaded pencil (#4) to draw the pattern so that the lines will be visible through the freezer paper when it's time to transfer the pattern for construction. Use a ruler for all straight lines and a flexible curve to help you draw curves. Keep a good, clean eraser handy. You may draft the pattern on a sheet of paper and then enlarge it to full size on a photocopier.

Another way to enlarge a pattern is by using grid paper. Begin by sketching it onto ¼″ (0.75 cm) graph paper. Then, square by square, copy the pattern onto 1″ (2.5 cm) grid paper, making sure that the lines of the pattern fall precisely into the corresponding grid boxes. The final drawing will be four times larger than the sketch. Grid paper is also available in larger sizes, or you can draft out your own according to your needs.

Alternatively, you can transfer the pattern from a small sheet of paper onto a transparency sheet using a transparency marking pen with a sharp point. You can then view the pattern with an overhead projector, casting the image onto a blank wall. Enlarge it to the size you require by turning the dial or, with older models, moving the projector back and forth. When the image is set to the correct size, tape a blank sheet of paper to the wall. Take a sharp pencil and trace the projected image onto the paper.

Marking Templates

Once your focal point(s) is drawn on your master pattern, you begin to see your pattern in terms of templates. Label each leaf, petal, or shape that makes up the focal point. Now you've identified the templates in your pattern.

Divide the Background into Templates

Once the elements of your composition are in place, turn your attention to the *negative space* on the rest of the paper. Decide whether you would prefer to use straight lines or curved lines to break up the background of the quilt top and connect the components of the pattern. These lines will ultimately form the templates that comprise the background of your quilt top. Use a ruler or flexible curve to add the lines to your master pattern. If it is compatible with your pattern and its focal point, try echoing the focal point shapes in the background. Common in music, echoing is an effective tool in art, too.

Another way to break up the background is by simply extending some of the lines that make up the focal design. In the sketch of *Spring Tulip* (page 94), I have continued the curve from the tip of the leaf, using a flexible curve. A single, graceful line now flows from the base of the leaf to its tip, extending off the edge of the design.

Continuing, I separated the background into templates that connected each of the leaves. Look at my sketch of the tulip. You will see that the tip of every petal or leaf is connected to another line or shape in the background of the pattern.

Blacklick Pond: Reflections at Twilight *detail. See the full quilt on page viii. Here the lily pad is echoed in the background.*

To unify the design, you must connect the positive spaces in the composition (tulip and leaves) with the negative space (background).

The simplest way to connect lines and points is to extend the existing lines off the edge of the design.

Draw new lines to connect all points and lines to some other line or shape.

You could also join the lines by drawing connecting lines at an angle to the points.

Fire Within *detail. See the full quilt on page 32. The spiral focal point is the most complex part of the pattern, since the curves are very tight and the templates that make it up extend into very fine points. Tackle these difficult areas first.*

Not only does this sense of connection make the pattern more pleasing artistically, but it also makes it much easier to construct the background templates. For example, a template covers the raw edges of each of those fine petal tips, giving a perfect point.

Notice how the overall effect changes when the background behind the tulip is broken up differently, as in the next sketch. Here, each point is still connected to another line in the pattern, but the flow is altogether different. The version will appear very different from the first one when made up in fabric.

There are, then, five key guidelines to remember when splitting up the background into templates:

- All areas of the pattern (focal point, other shapes, and background) must be connected to each other.
- Every line in the pattern must be connected.
- Every point in the pattern must be connected to another line or shape in the background.
- The lines that you draw in the background must divide that area into distinct shapes that are easy to make up into templates.
- Each background shape should vary in appearance and mass size and be aesthetically pleasing but should not overpower the focal point.

Numbering the Templates

As you discovered when you made *Spring Tulip* in Chapter 1 or any of the projects in Chapter 2, the numbering of the templates, which indicates the sequence in which they will be sewn, is very important.

Every master pattern has more than one possible starting place. To number the templates of your pattern, you can begin at the center of the project or in any corner. Begin by looking over your pattern very carefully, identifying areas that seem more complex than others. In particular, look for sharp points and tight curves.

Use the following guidelines to help you decide how to sequence your template:

1. Identify the sharp, narrow points in the design. To create an effortless, perfect point, you must figure the sequence so that the point is sandwiched between the template that lies beneath it and the one that will lie on top of it. This allows you to sew even the narrowest tips accurately. In this sketch, template A would be put in place first. Template B is second. Its turned-under seam covers the raw edges of A. The narrow tip of the tulip leaf is created by overlapping the raw seam allowance of B with a succeeding template, C.

2. Plan the sequence so that you are turning under seams for concave (inward) curves rather than convex (outward) ones. The reason is that concave curves are much easier to make. For example, in the pattern *Spiral Daisy* (page 31), the sequence is numbered so you are piecing only concave curves. This enables you to put this pattern together faster and easier than if it were set up in the opposite direction (piecing convex curves).

3. Look for areas of the design where as many as four or five angled templates butt up against a single template. If possible, use the single template to cover the raw edges of the others. The long, unbroken lines of a single template give a smoother look to the project after it is stitched.

Look at the two drawings here and try to determine how best to number the templates for easy construction. Number each piece in sequence and add small arrows to indicate which seam allowances you would turn under. On each

Step 1. Sandwich narrow, sharp points such as the one in template B between other templates for easy construction. Consider these sharp points first when numbering the templates for your pattern.

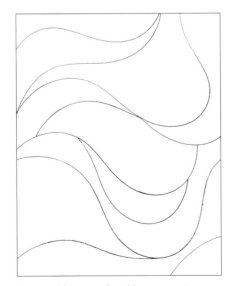

How would you number this wavy master pattern for easy construction? Since most of the piecing is of concave (inward) curves, numbering is quite easy.

How would you number this angled master pattern for easy contruction?

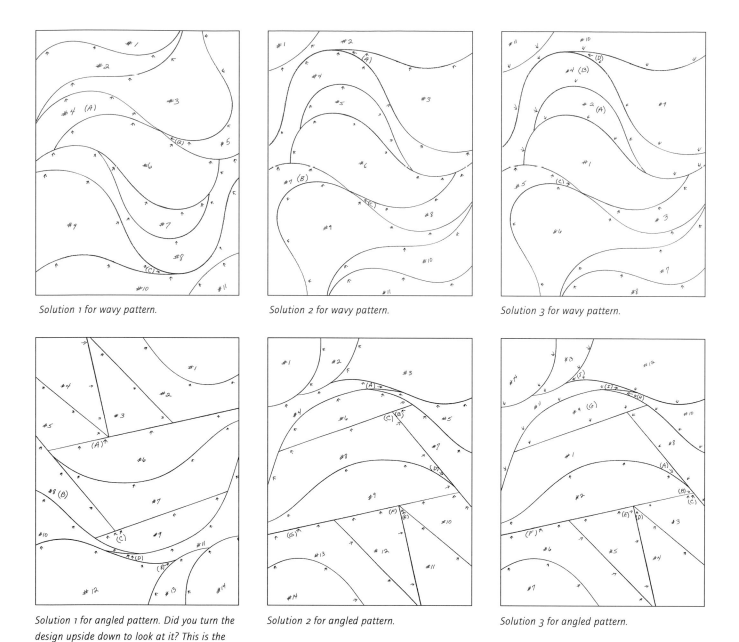

Solution 1 for wavy pattern.

Solution 2 for wavy pattern.

Solution 3 for wavy pattern.

Solution 1 for angled pattern. Did you turn the design upside down to look at it? This is the easiest solution.

Solution 2 for angled pattern.

Solution 3 for angled pattern.

page, I have provided three possible "solutions" for each of the two patterns. The solutions for the wavy pattern are:

1. (A) The order of templates 4 and 5 is interchangeable. (B) The trimmed seam allowance from the tip of template 5 needs to be angled back and folded beneath itself so that it evenly abuts the top of template 4 and is covered by template 6. (C) This narrow point must be sandwiched between templates 8 and 10.

2. (A) The narrow point of template 3 must be sandwiched between templates 2 and 4. (B) The order of templates 7 and 8 is interchangeable. (C) The trimmed seam allowance from the tip of template 8 must be angled back and folded beneath itself so it evenly abuts the tip of template 7 and is covered by template 9.

3. (A) The order of templates 2 and 3 is interchangeable. (B) Template 4 covers templates 1, 2, and 3. (C) The trimmed seam allowance from the tip of template 5 needs to be angled back and folded beneath itself so that it evenly abuts the top of template 3 and is covered by template 6. (D) The narrow point of template 9 must be sandwiched between templates 4 and 10.

The solutions for the angled pattern are:

1. (A) The straight line of template 6 covers all the angles and points of templates 2 through 5. (B) Template 8 covers the short side of template 5 and the narrow points of templates 6 and 7. (C) Template 9 covers template 7 and the short side and narrow angle of template 8. (D) The narrow point of template 10 must be sandwiched between templates 9 and 11. The narrow point of template 11 must be sandwiched between templates 10 and 12. (E) The narrow point of template 12 must be sandwiched between templates 11 and 13.

2. (A) The narrow point of template 4 must be sandwiched between templates 3 and 5. The narrow point of template 5 must be sandwiched between templates 4 and 6. (B and C) Angle B is much narrower or more acute than angle C. Since it is easier to form obtuse angles, template 7 comes first so that its narrow angle is covered up by template 8. (D) The narrow point of template 8 must be sandwiched between templates 7 and 9. (E) The trimmed seam allowance from the tip of template 11 must be angled back and folded beneath itself so it is covered by the corner of template 12. (F) As it is stitched down, all the points and angles of templates 10 through 13 must form a straight line.

3. (A, B, and C) Narrow points and angles of templates 1 through 3 are easier to construct if they are covered by a succeeding template, in this case template 8. (D) The trimmed seam allowance from the tips of templates 3 and 4 are covered by the wide, obtuse angle E of template 5. (E) Since it is easier to form obtuse angles, the narrow tips of templates 3 and 4 are covered by the wide, obtuse angle E of template 5. (F) As you stitch line F, take care that all points and angles of templates 3 through 6 form a straight line. (G) Template 9 covers template 1 and the short, narrow angle of template 8. (H and I) The narrow point of template 10 must be sandwiched between templates 9 and 11. The narrow point of template 11 is sandwiched between templates 9, 10, and 12. (J) The narrow point of template 12 must be sandwiched between templates 11 and 13.

Learning what to look for and how to number the templates is not difficult, but it does take some practice. You should number the templates on several quilts until you get the hang of sequence. After that, you'll be able to figure out the piecing order as you make the quilt. I usually start numbering on the master pattern either at the top left corner or at the focal point. I choose the focal point if the design involves a lot of complex piecing. I start at the center of the focal point and work outward toward the edges of the quilt. Remember that simplicity is essential. Keep your first efforts easy and gradually build up to more complex designs.

Choosing Colors

One of the most enjoyable experiences for a quilter is choosing the colors and prints for a quilt. Color is all around us: a bright rainbow on a rainy day, vivid orange leaves against a brilliant blue sky, and a colorful riot of mixed wildflowers. Color affects our attitude and our soul, and it is the tool we use to paint our feeling into our quilts. It would take an entire book to discuss the subject of color, and there are many excellent educational books about color available. Several are written especially for quiltmaking. In this section I would like to share with you some of my thoughts about my favorite subject—color!

Color Terms

Following is a list of color terms used throughout the book, which define the characteristics of color. Knowing these characteristics will help you choose colors when you shop for fabric.

- Color—Our eyes' perception of the way light is reflected. Our color sensations vary constantly depending on the type of light reflected, how that light changes, and the other colors that surround it.
- Hue—A word that defines a color, for example, *red*, *reddish purple*, *bluish green*, *yellow*, *blue*, *orange*, and so on.
- Saturation or intensity (chroma)—The vividness or purity of a hue. The purer the hue, the higher the intensity. The more a hue is diluted with white, gray, or black, the lower the intensity.
- Tint—A pure hue with white added.
- Shade—A pure hue with black added.
- Tone—A pure hue with gray added.
- Contrast of color—A noticeable difference in color or value when compared or seen from a distance.
- Value—The lightness or darkness of a hue on a scale from white to black. The color on the light end of the scale (white) is a high value. The color on the black end of the scale is a low value.
- Relativity of value—How a color appears to change depending on its position next to or surrounded by other colors.
- Cool color—One perceived as cool to the eye, such as blue, green, and purple. The more blue in the color, the cooler it appears.
- Warm color—One perceived as warm to the eye such as red, orange, and yellow. The more yellow or red in a color, the warmer it appears.

Thinking About Color

Uncertainty and indecision with color choices is probably the scariest dilemma the quiltmaker faces. It needn't be so. Learn to love and enjoy all colors and the joy they bring into your life. Relax. The fact is that the more you play around with color and have fun with it, the less intimidating it becomes. Be free to experiment, for it is only through working with color that you will gain confidence.

Fire and Ice *detail is an example of combining warm and cool colors. See the full quilt on page 14.*

Creation of the Sun and Stars *detail is an example of color balance. Incorporate focal point color, in this case red, into the background templates.*

Creation of the Sun and Stars *detail shows the use of light and dark colors. See the full quilt on page 84.*

The following guidelines reflect my personal approach to color. I try to keep them in mind as I plan and make my quilts.

• Judge colors from a distance. When you shop for fabrics or while you are piecing the quilt top, stand 10 to 20 feet (3 to 6 meters) away to see how they will look. Colors that look great up close may lose their zing when hanging on a wall across the room. The opposite is true, too. Colors that clash horribly when seen close-up can thrill you when they are 15 feet away. Judge by eye only; peepholes do not give accurate assessments.

• Look at color combinations; don't focus on a single color. Your quilt may combine many hues, so consider the effect of the colors you've chosen as a whole; do not consider colors individually. Look at the world around you and learn from nature. All colors can and do work together to form beauty.

• Seek color contrast. Contrast is a necessary ingredient for a stunning quilt. A quilt with too much similarity in color, value, or brightness merely hums. If you want your quilt to sing, you must add contrast. For maximum visual impact, vary the values (light to dark) and intensity (brightness) of color in your quilt. Use vibrant colors against tones and shades. A little clash adds interest, too.

• Use color strategy. Think about colors and color combinations before you begin a quilt. What colors are best for the mood you want to create? Which colors will make the focal point dominant? Which colors will help the background recede? Remember that the focal point should stand out both in design and color. The highest color contrast, value, and brightness should be at the focal point of your quilt, diminishing as the eye travels away.

• Combine warm and cool colors. Cool colors such as green, blue, and purple recede into the background. Warm colors, such as red, orange, and yellow, come to the foreground and catch the eye first. Visually, yellow is the most powerful color. Red is the most emotionally provocative one. Warm colors are dominant and stimulating, so be wary of using them excessively. Temper them with cool colors to avoid overpowering the quilt top. The opposite is also true—too many cool colors need a spark of warm color to add excitement. Keep in mind that color temperature is relative. How a color reads depends on the color it is

To open yourself up to new ideas about using color, I heartily recommend that you invite several other quilting friends over to your house for a "colorfest" session. Ask each person to bring odd, wild, and colorful scraps of fabric for sharing, white poster board, and temporary adhesive spray. Use the poster board as a foundation to make the improvisational fabric mock-ups of a simple pattern. Glue the fabric to the poster board with adhesive spray or other fabric adhesive. Each person should bring a sheet of foam core board to use as a portable design wall. Secure the board with drafting tape to a wall in the room or prop it up against a worktable. View the color choices from a distance and explore the unlimited color possibilities together as a group.

In friendly group settings you'll be more daring to interact, play, and experiment, like you did as children. Avoid using the safe colors you normally use in your quilts. If you don't like the colors and combinations you used in your mock-up, rework the design or throw it away. Chances are that you will be very pleased with your experimental quilt and with yourself as well.

next to. Normally, green is considered a cool color. But positioned side by side, a green with a tinge of yellow appears warmer than either a bluish green or even a dark shade of red. But the same green placed next to pure yellow or red will seem cooler.

• Try to achieve color balance. Too many vivid, saturated colors can overpower a quilt. Adding tones and shades subdues the intensity and helps you achieve a pleasant balance. Toned colors enhance vivid colors and make them glow. The opposite is also true; too many toned colors are boring, so add some intense, vivid colors for interest. Improve balance by incorporating into the background the tones and shades of colors you used for the focal point. For example, if your project has fire, think about using a fabric that has a touch or hint of a red shade somewhere else in the background of the quilt.

• Include very dark and very light colors in your quilt. These will help show off the medium values that most of us favor. Colors will appear more vibrant against a dark background. Instead of using plain black, which can be cold or impersonal, substitute other hues, such as deep purple, navy, or blackish green.

• Don't forget the background! Take as much care in choosing background colors as you do in choosing colors for your focal point. Remember that light and warm colors come forward; cool and dark colors recede.

• Daylight, especially morning light, is the best and truest light source to use when choosing colors for your quilt. Our impressions of color change according to the lighting we see them in. Incandescent, fluorescent, tungsten, and halogen lighting, for example, can impart a yellow, blue, or orange cast to a fabric. There is lighting available that simulates daylight, which is very helpful when the real source is not available. Check for these special light bulbs at home improvement stores and shops that specialize in lighting fixtures.

• Most of the fabrics in a quilt shop are in colors of medium value. These are the fabrics that catch our eye and that we purchase most often. To show off these medium-value fabrics to their best advantage, they must be contrasted with dark and light fabrics. These fabrics are harder to find. Make a special effort to look for and pick up those great dark- and light-colored fabrics for your stash when you come across them.

• Work with all colors, even ones you don't like. At the least, learn to tolerate them in your work—they all have a purpose.

Starting today, notice the colors in your world. How do you relate to them? Study the colors in nature, and then relax and play. Allow the artistry in you to flow freely and without worry. Discover that creativity is fun!

Don't agonize over color choices. Usually, your instinctive color preferences are the correct ones. If you simply cannot make a color decision while working on a quilt, set it aside until later when you can look at it with a fresh eye.

Achieving Visual Depth

You can make the focal point of your quilt top stand out from the background by giving your quilt visual depth. In a quilt that has *visual depth*, some elements of the

After the Storm, 1997, 57″ × 62″
(145 cm × 167 cm).
This quilt is a sequel to Breaking
Point *and was made to celebrate my
husband's recovery from cancer; its
theme is hope. During times when
our personal storms and crises batter
and beat us down, we are sustained
by the strong roots of faith and the
trust that the storm will pass and
the skies will clear. After the storm
passes, we look to the horizon once
more for a life filled with happiness
and serenity.*

pattern come forward to meet the eye, while others recede into the background. There are several techniques you can use to achieve visual depth in your quilts.

Careful manipulation of color, tones, and shades is one way to achieve visual depth. You can use several different color values or you can use graduated colors. For instance, suppose you wish to add depth to a pattern containing a tree. By mixing tints, deep shades, tones, and pure hues of green you will give the illusion of depth because the lighter tints come forward and the deep shades recede.

Another way to achieve depth is through manipulation of line perspective and color. In the landscape shown in *Resting Place*, for example, the winding stream has visual depth. The templates at the head of the stream are very narrow. As the stream rushes forward, the templates grow wider. This gives the illusion of movement as well as depth. The use of graduating colors, beginning with just a tint of blue for the first template and graduating through light tones to vivid blue to deep blue, adds to this illusion.

Similarly, you can achieve depth by increasing or decreasing the size of a shape. The larger the shape, the more intense the color; and the more the contrast within a shape, the closer it appears to be. A smaller shape with dulled color and less contrast will recede into the background.

Resting Place. *See the full quilt on page 46.*

Resting Place. *See the full quilt on page 46.*

Careful use of line and color suggests the leaf is folding back over itself.

Overlapping shapes also gives an impression of depth. You can overlap lines to give the impression that one object is lying on top of another. This effect is easily enhanced by color choices. In this quilt detail, the lighter template at the front overlaps three darker templates. The illusion is that the leaf is folded over itself.

Piecing Large Quilt Tops

I construct my quilts by tracing, piecing, and sewing down one section of templates at a time, matching each section to the previous one until I finish the entire quilt. As the completed surface grows, I enlarge the stabilizer foundation as needed by fusing on another strip to the existing one.

Begin piecing a large quilt by tackling the most complex area first. This is usually the focal point. Break down the master pattern into smaller segments, each made up of approximately ten to fifteen templates. Trace these templates onto freezer paper and pin the freezer paper onto the stabilizer. Piece, sew, and press the first section.

Choose a neighboring area for the next section of templates and trace them onto freezer paper. Include and mark on your tracing any distinctive angles, sharp narrow points, or peculiar seam intersections from the previous section of templates. You can accurately position the new section of freezer-paper templates to the quilt by matching the traced "landmarks" to the actual sewn angles, points, and seams in the first section. Once you are satisfied the placement is correct, pin the freezer paper in place and construct as usual.

When you piece a large quilt in segments, there will be templates that are literally left hanging. Their seams are turned under, but you cannot completely sew them down until templates from the next section are in place. Pin down any unstitched edges to the stabilizer so that they hold their crease and are ready to fit in once the next segment of the pattern is under way.

Once you are comfortable figuring the numerical sequence of the templates, you don't need to mark every template before you begin a large quilt. You can figure the order and piece templates for each section as the work progresses.

It's helpful if you can continue to piece in the same general direction, that is, if you turn under the seams on the same side(s) of each successive template.

Making Adjustments

Particularly with larger quilts, problems of accuracy arise, no matter how carefully you have sewn. Sometimes, a new section of templates does not match up perfectly with the seams you have already pieced. This is common as you near the end of the project and construction is almost complete. One of the most appealing aspects of topstitch piecing is that it is easy to make adjustments as you go. All you need to do when you find a template does not match a previously sewn piece is either trim or add to that template so that it fits.

To trim a template, first match it up to the corresponding section of the design to which you will sew. Use paper scissors to trim the edge of the freezer-paper template so that it fits.

To extend the template, use drafting tape to build up the edge. Sometimes, the adjustment is so slight that all you need to do is wrap a small piece of tape around the edge of the freezer paper so that it sticks to both the dull and shiny sides. You can then trim the tape with paper scissors for an exact fit. For bigger adjustments, use drafting tape to attach a new piece of freezer paper to the existing template, and then trim it back to fit.

Reversing the Direction of Turned-Under Seam Allowances

Especially with larger projects, it is tough to plan out the numbering sequence, and sometimes you will need to make adjustments while you are sewing. For example, you may find that you have narrow points or raw edges to cover, but the flow of the template sequence is heading in the wrong direction! If you are caught in this situation, you can escape by using this easy technique to reverse direction. (Keep in mind that the example shown is for teaching purposes. You will be using this technique on the quilt surface. At least one of the templates will probably already be pinned or partially sewn down.)

• On the freezer paper make a straight hash mark on the common seam line of the two templates involved. A convenient spot midway is fine.

• Make a straight cut into the fabric (to the edge of the freezer paper) at the hash mark on both templates.

• Split the seam allowance in two. Turn under the section on which you need to reverse direction and cover the raw point, but leave the other half as a flat, raw edge.

• Prepare the second template exactly the opposite. The raw edge half of the second template corresponds with the turned edge of the first template, and the turned edge of the second template corresponds with the raw edge of the first template.

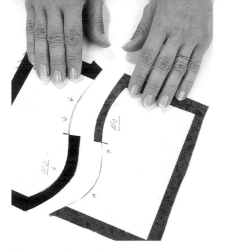

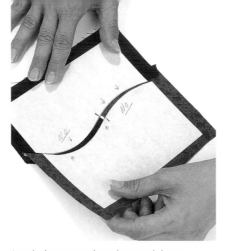

Sometimes the numbering system can go awry when you are joining several sections of a large quilt. This simple technique of reversing the direction of turned-under seam allowances on two templates has saved me many times.

Interlock two templates in a straight cut, nudging the raw allowance of each template beneath the turned-under allowance of the other.

Blindstitch each turned seam down, using your sewing machine's mirror image stitching feature or stitching from the cut outward in each direction.

• Intersect the two templates at the cut, and fit the raw edges of each template beneath the turned seam of the other. Adjust so they fit closely, and pin and remove the freezer paper.

• Blindstitch an overlapped seam to the hash mark and backstitch one stitch to lock. If your sewing machine has a mirror image, reverse stitch direction and blindstitch the remaining seam. If your machine does not have mirror image, turn the project around and blindstitch the remaining seam. The reversal is invisible to the eye.

This is an important maneuver to remember—it will get you out of many a scrape!

Improvisational Quilts

One of the most exciting ways to use the topstitch piecing technique is to make improvisational quilt tops, designing as you go. As the name implies, this type of quilt is created without a pattern and with fabrics you have on hand. Impromptu work is stress free and liberating. The quilt takes on a life of its own, and you never quite know how it is going to turn out until it is finished. There are no instuctions to follow, so you do not need to be precise. Best of all, you can do just as you please with color and placement of shapes. It is a wonderful way to experiment freely with color. While some of my quilts have taken me as long as five or six months to complete, I can finish an improvised quilt in anywhere from two days to two weeks.

Stay flexible when you encounter sharp points in your pattern. Keep in mind that this is improvisation. If you can't manipulate the point easily or fudge on the angle, cover it up with the seam of another fabric template! Anything goes, and that is why this is a stress-free method.

As you work, remember to keep a good color balance, contrasts, and values in the quilt. View the project from a distance to determine which colors or values you need to balance the next section of the quilt. For example, if you have orange fabric in one area, include orange in other areas of the quilt for color balance.

Since improvisational piecing is done on impulse, there are no set rules. You may reinvent traditional pattern blocks, as I did in *Celebrate Until Midnight* and *Pond Reflections at Dawn* (page 107), or simply experiment using unusual shapes and colorful fabric scraps. In the pages that follow, I explain how I made several improvisational quilts. I hope these will inspire you to use similar techniques to create free-flow quilts of your own.

Mayhem in My Garden

I finished this quilt in only two days, and it was very simple to construct. The inspiration came when I looked outside and saw a tangle of weeds and flowers growing together in the garden.

I cut the floral iris fabric into 5″ × 21″ (13 cm × 53 cm) strips and turned under seam allowances of about ⅜″ (1 cm) on both long edges of the strip. I made the other strips from navy blue batik fabric and pieced them with 1½″ (4 cm) strips of green and rust at various odd angles. If I made this quilt again, I would vary the width of the green and orange strips. After I completed the piecing on the blue/green/rust strip, I trimmed it to a 5″ (13 cm) strip also. I did not turn under these edges.

I alternated the strips and carefully arranged them on the stabilizer foundation. I covered the raw edges of the pieced blue strips with the floral strips with the turned allowances. I pinned the strips together on the stabilizer, sewed them

down, and pressed. At this point, I squared up the quilt and marked it with a quilt marking pencil to make a perfect rectangle.

I added the ¾″ (2 cm) inner border (see page 52). I pieced the outside border with navy and the floral fabric (1½″ [3.75 cm] strips) at uneven angles and cut it into strips 5″ (13 cm) wide plus the length of each side of the quilt. I added a third border, a 1″ (2.5 cm) green, to the quilt and made it in the same way as the inner borders. I used the rust color for the quilt binding.

The free-motion stitching combines a geometric pattern to represent the weeds and echo quilting on the flowers and leaves. I mimicked the iris, continuing the outline of the flower in thread from the floral fabric onto the navy background (see page 73). I did the same with some of the leaves, extending the leaf stitching design onto the neighboring strips of fabric.

Pond Reflections at Dawn

I made this quilt entirely with scraps and discarded fabric templates. I decided on a triangular shape and experimented to replicate the style of a log cabin block, but with a curved touch. As I began to work, I found that instead of making the traditional four-sided log cabin block, a three-sided block worked out better with curves. Additionally, the three-sided block was in keeping with the basic triangle shape. I included fabrics that were in keeping with a pond theme, such as those with butterflies and fish in the print.

I formed each block by starting with a small piece of fabric for the center that was very dark. The center piece was surrounded on three sides with fabrics in a medium value. I cut pieces of fabric and turned under their edge or edges at random to create the seam allowances. I tried to incorporate as many curved seams as possible. This was a great opportunity to recycle unneeded fabric templates from previous projects and to use up fabric in my scrap pile.

When the fabric had a straight edge that I wanted to make curved, I cut along the edge in a slight concave (inward) arc, turned under the seam, and pressed. I made slight clips in the seam allowance as necessary for a smooth turn. For convex (outward) curves, I cut the fabric edge in an outward arc, trimmed to $\frac{1}{4}''$ (0.75 cm), and turned under, making the arc as sharp or as gentle as needed to cover the raw edges of the center fabric.

For the third group of templates, I chose a color value darker than the middle group, but in most cases not as dark as the center fabric. The number of sides for the third set of templates varied. I used three strips of fabric for most blocks, but sometimes I needed four strips to complete the block. I pieced an entire block before sewing down the seams using the machine blindstitch.

I began piecing the quilt in the middle of a large sheet of stabilizer and worked outward. I constructed many of the blocks directly on the stabilizer. In some areas I had difficulty getting blocks to fit properly with that method. For those blocks, I used sheet waxed paper as a foundation. I constructed each block

Pond Reflections at Dawn, 2000, 61″ × 76½″ × 76½″ (155 cm × 194 cm × 194 cm).
This triangular quilt is an improvisational, abstract scene from Blacklick Pond. It is my unrestricted and curvy interpretation of log cabin blocks.

on a piece of waxed paper and, when finished, carefully removed the paper from the backside of the block. I pressed the block well to flatten and stretch it before I turned under appropriate edges and added it to the other blocks already sewn to the stabilizer.

I made up three or four blocks at a time before attaching them to the quilt. Each block comes together differently, and because of the diversity in size, some blocks will fit better in certain areas than others. Having several blocks to choose from for the perfect fit is helpful. Sometimes, when I could not get a good fit, I added long wedges to take up the extra space between blocks.

I built the quilt to a triangular shape and then cut it to its exact size with a rotary cutter and mat. I used a loose meandering free-motion stitch to simulate the ripples in water.

Sunrise

I pieced this quilt top similar to the way I pieced *Pond Reflections at Dawn*, piecing each block separately on waxed paper and then arranging it on the stabilizer foundation. I cut the black sashing symbolizing my window into strips with a rotary cutter. I cut the strips with curved edges. Although the width of the sashing strips varied because of the random curves, I made sure the strips were no less than 2″ (5 cm) wide at any point. This was to allow for a ½″ (1.5 cm) turned-under seam allowance on both long edges of the sashing I would use between the four blocks.

I worked on the left side blocks first, positioning the black sashing between the top and bottom blocks. The topstitch allowance of the sashing covered the raw edges of both blocks. I pinned the sashing and blocks in place on the stabilizer. Likewise, I put the blocks for the right side in place along with the sashing separating them and pinned them. I positioned the center sashing separating the right and left sets of blocks next. The turned seams of the center sashing covered the raw edges of all four blocks. I made some adjustments, such as moving the blocks in a bit closer and using another section of sashing that matches a little better. Once the center sashing was in place, I sewed down the sashing and blocks to the stabilizer and pressed well.

I added black sashing one side at a time around the outside of the four blocks to complete the window illusion. For the outside sashing, I turned under only one long edge of the strip for a seam allowance, which covers the blocks. The outside border covers the raw edge of this sashing. I mitered the corners at any angle that was easy to manipulate.

I pieced the colorful outside border directly onto the stabilizer. I turned under the fabric edges and arranged them so that the border pieces covered the raw edges of the black sashing. I pinned them down, and when I was satisfied with the placement, stitched them in place. I squared and trimmed the quilt top, allowing room for a wide binding.

I cut the binding in strips, measuring the lengths to accommodate the sides (see page 58, Step 2). I cut the strips straight on one side and curved on the other, similar to the sashing. I made sure not to cut the width less than 3″ (7.6 cm) at any point. I turned under the seam allowance on the curvy edges and attached

Sunrise, 1996, 31″ × 31″
(79 cm × 79 cm).
*A spectacular October sunrise I
witnessed from my bedroom window
was the inspiration for this quilt. The
colors were so incredible I went
immediately to my workroom to pick
out fabrics that matched the shades
in the morning sky.*

the binding one side at a time, starting with the left and right sides and then top and bottom. The width of the binding showing on the surface ranges from ³/₄″ to 2¹/₂″ (2 cm to 6.4 cm). I turned the excess binding to the back, turned the raw edges under, and whipstitched it.

I added a rounded area of dense and random free-motion stitching using gold metallic ribbon threads depicting the sun on the lower right side of the quilt. The remaining stitching is flames angling outward in diagonal lines away from the rising sun.

Lilacs and Lace

This fun and fast quilt was easy to make. I pieced and blindstitched this quilt directly on the stabilizer. I turned under the seam allowances on each fabric piece and arranged them to cover the raw edges of previous templates. For accent, I added snippets of lace on top of some fabric templates or in corners of others. I used small, round lace doilies of different diameters. I cut the doilies in quarters or whatever angle I needed, allowing for seam allowances. The seams of other pieces covered all the raw edges of the lace. I tried to keep a finished edge showing on the surface to prevent raveling. To secure the lace, I stitched it down along the scalloped edges using cream thread and a small straight stitch.

Lilacs and Lace, 1997, 27″ × 27″ (68 cm × 68 cm)

I made 2½″ (6.25 cm) squares for each of the four corners from the black velvet overlaid with lace. The lilac border's finished size is 2½″ (6.25 cm) (the raw border strip was cut to 3½″, or 8.75 cm). Because the velvet and lace seam allowance would be too bulky to turn under, I turned the lilac border seams instead. I adjusted the ½″ (1.25 cm) border seam allowance to fit correctly both on the side of the quilt and on the velvet corners and stitched the border with a blindstitch.

I sandwiched the finished quilt top with batting and inexpensive backing fabric. Instead of quilting, I used a variety of decorative stitches to cover the blindstitches around the patches. A walking foot is helpful in making sure all of the layers feed evenly through the needle. I made sure that the decorative stitches were centered over the seam and reached into both templates. I stopped and started decorative stitching approximately ¼″ to ⅜″ (0.75 cm to 1 cm) from seam intersections so that the different stitches would not overlap. I didn't use decorative stitching on the scalloped lace edges.

Not wanting any bobbin threads from the decorative stitching to show on the backside of my finished quilt, I added another backing of black fabric to hide the original backing after I finished the stitching. I pressed the new backing well and basted it to the back of the quilt sandwich on all four edges to assure a flat fit. I bound the quilt using a black ½″ (1.25 cm) French appliqué binding.

Templates

T he following pattern templates for each quilt top are full sized. Most patterns are divided among several pages. Each page is marked with the pattern's name and its position in the pattern's design.

To use the templates, trace each page of the pattern on a separate piece of paper and mark its position in the design (i.e., top right, bottom left). Then trace the dashed-line borders (_ _ _ _).

Once you have traced all pages of the pattern, trim the paper close to the dashed borders. On a table, place each page into the correct design position, overlapping the pages and matching up the dashed lines. Adjust and straighten the pages until the dashed lines coincide, using clear tape to join the pages. Once the master pattern is complete it may be traced onto freezer paper. Save the pattern for future use. You may enlarge the pattern on a photocopier if you desire a larger quilt top.

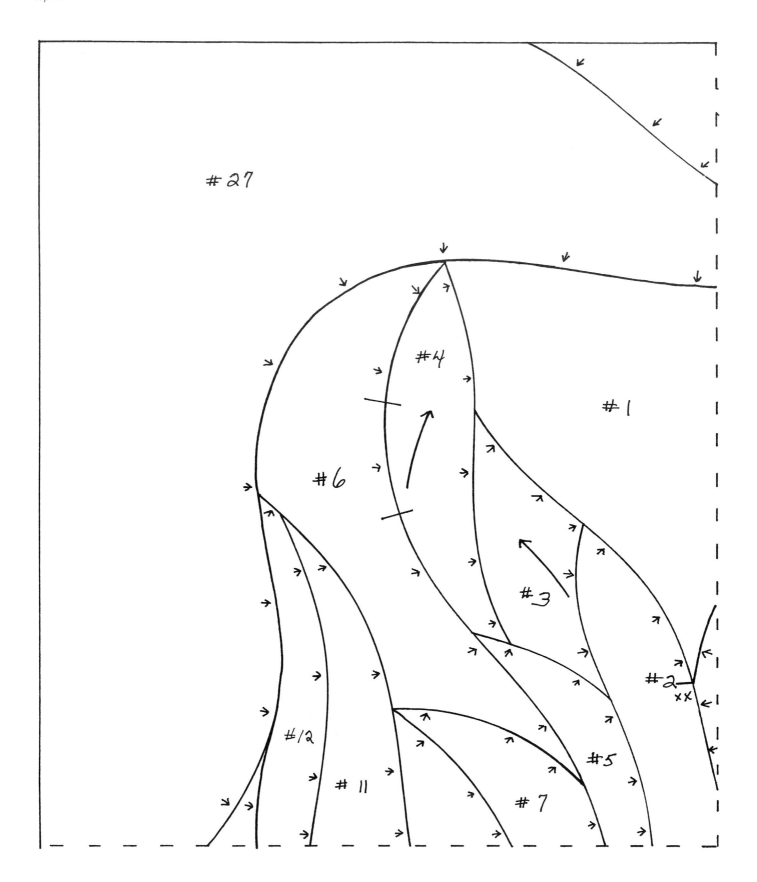

#27

#1

#4

#6

#3

#2
×x

#12

#11

#5

#7

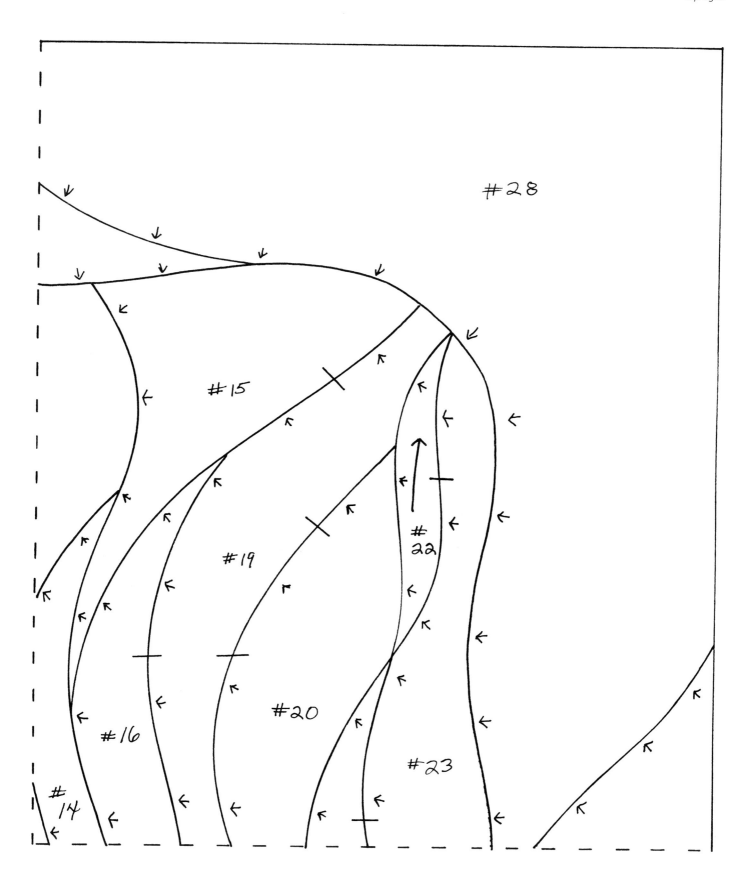

#28

#15

#19

#22

#16

#20

#23

#14

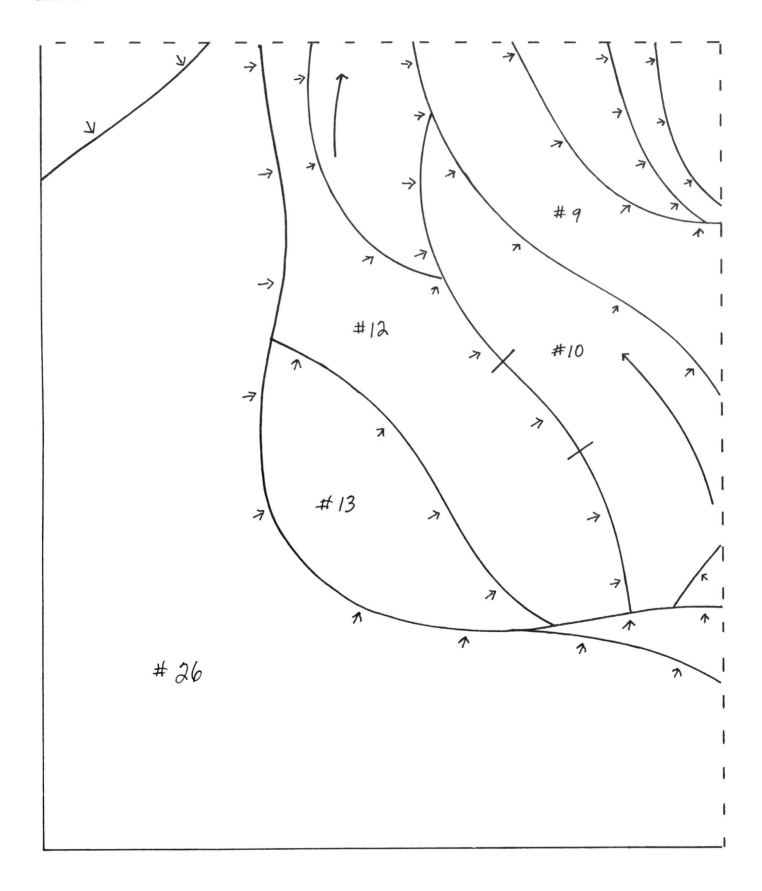

#9

#12

#10

#13

26

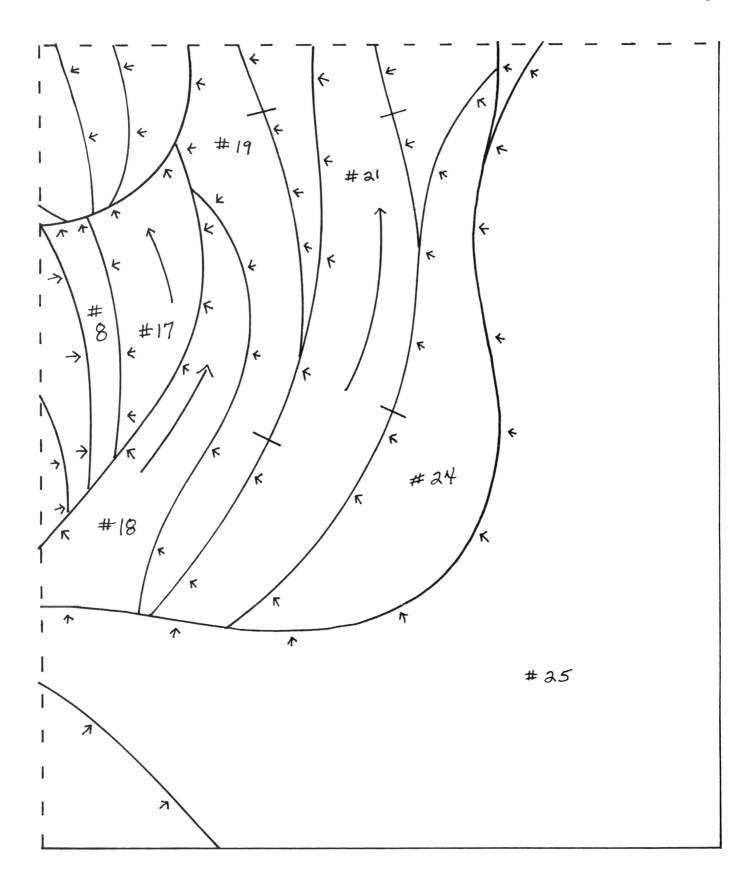

#19

#21

#8

#17

#18

#24

#25

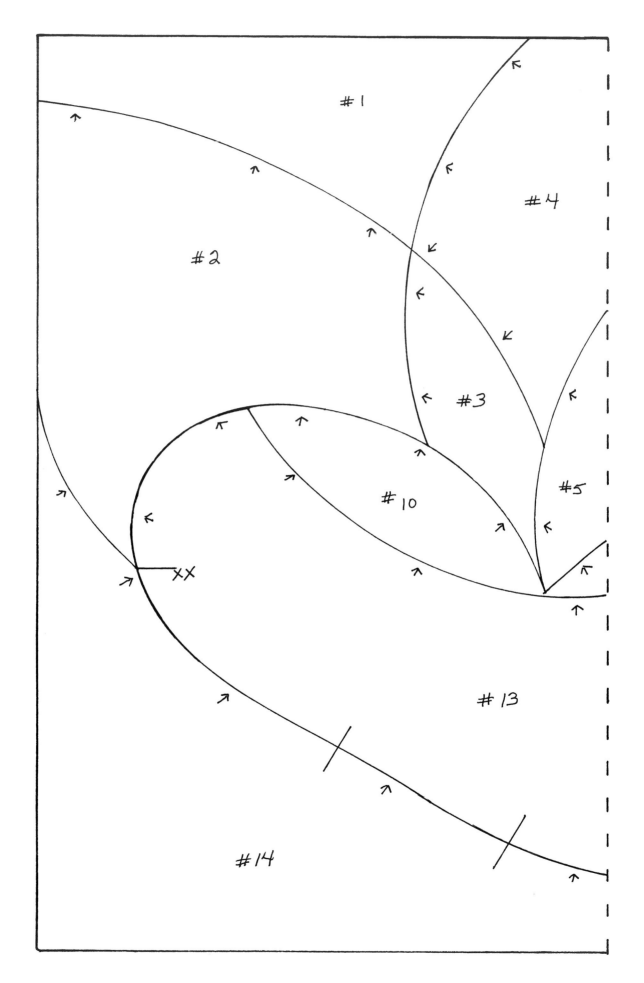

#1

#4

#2

#3

#10

#5

XX

#13

#14

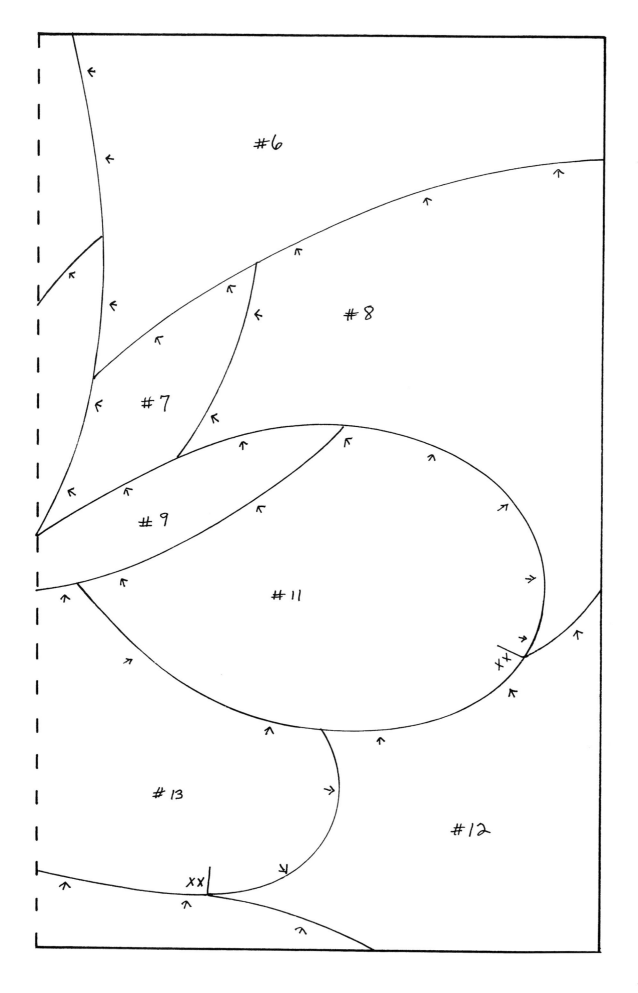

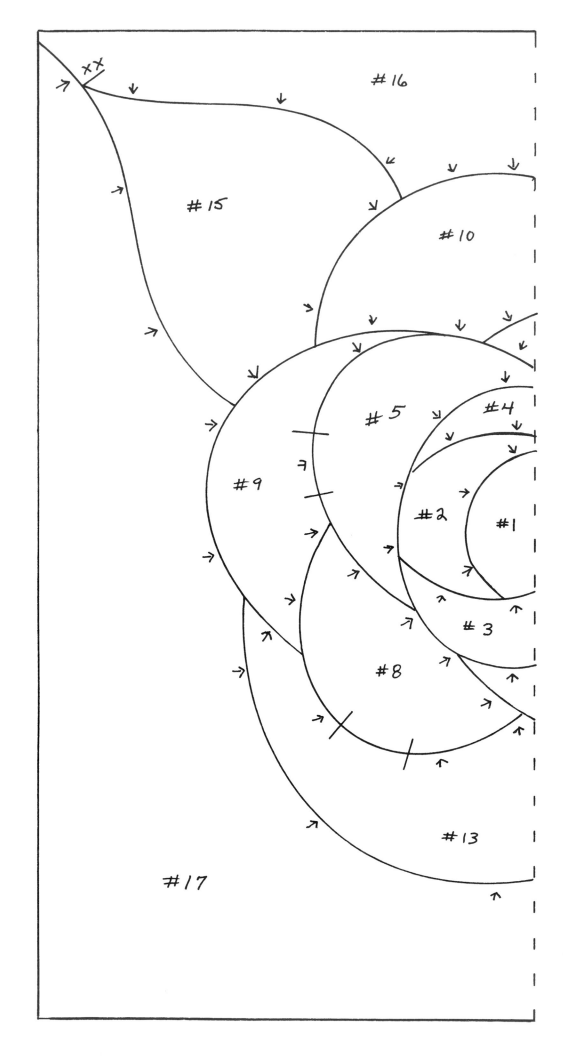

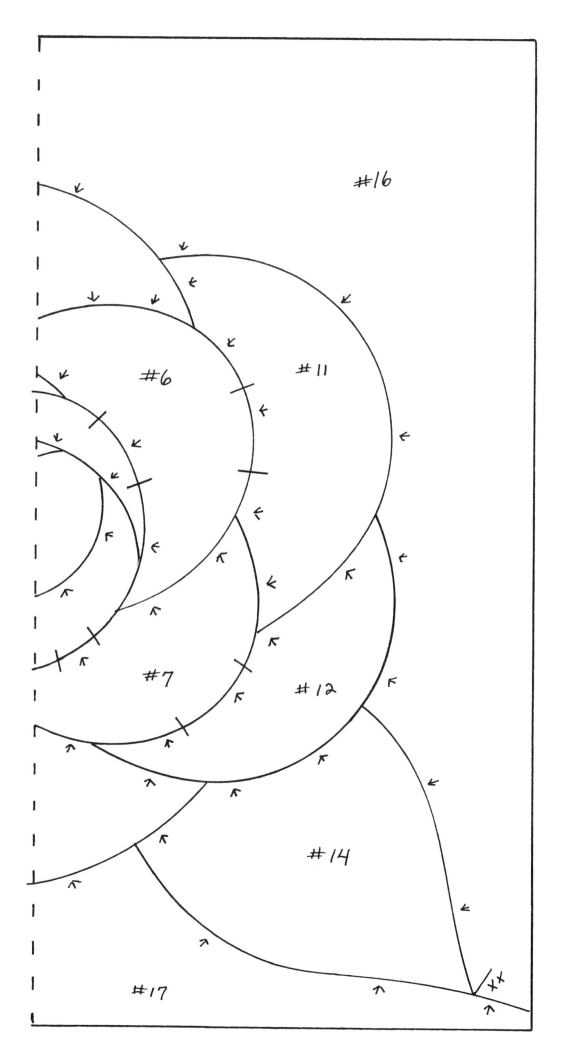

#16

#6

#11

#7

#12

#14

#17

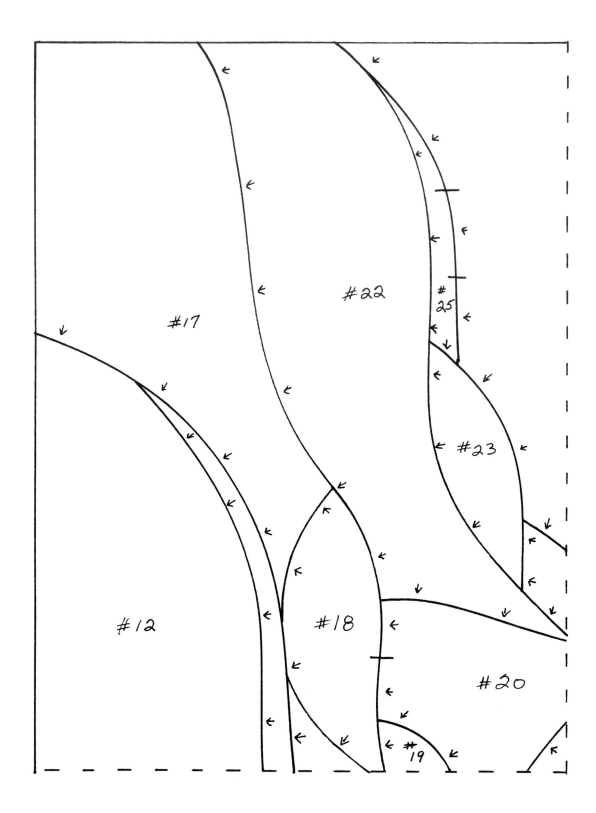

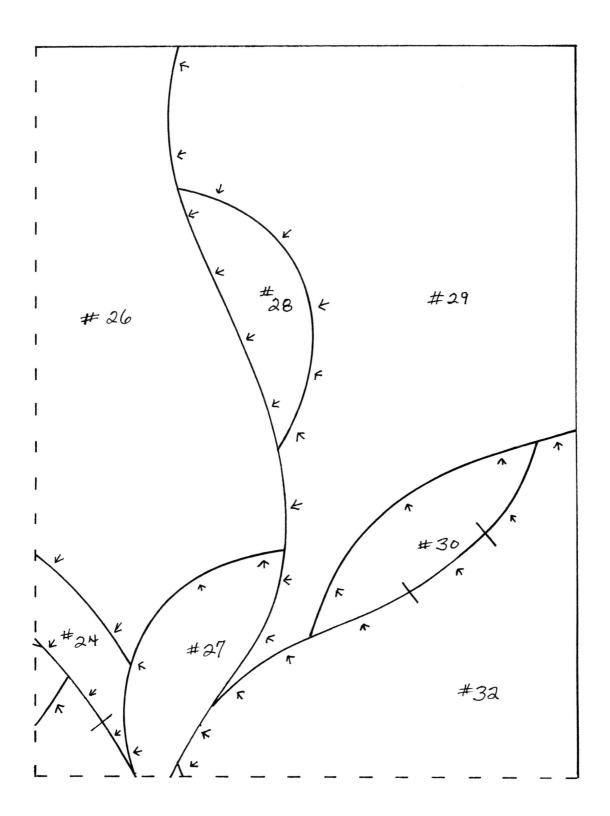

#26

#28

#29

#24

#27

#30

#32

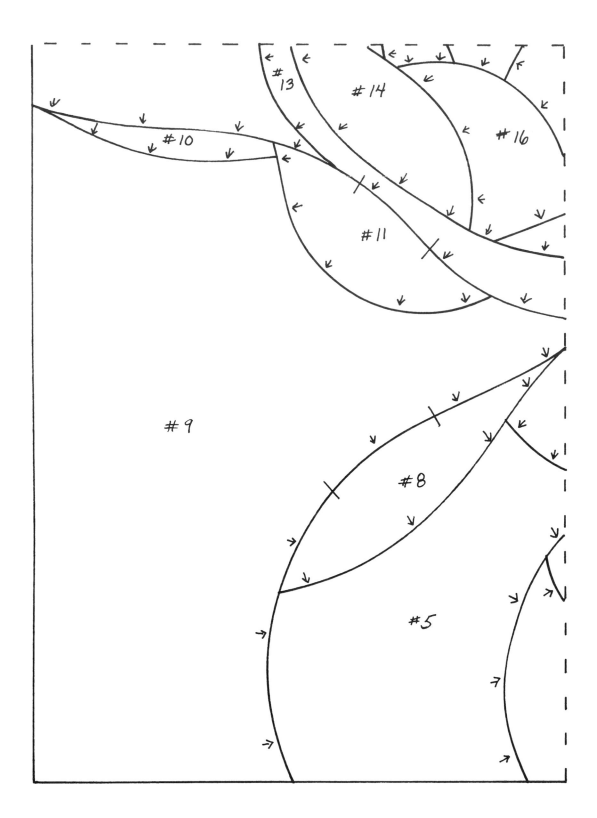

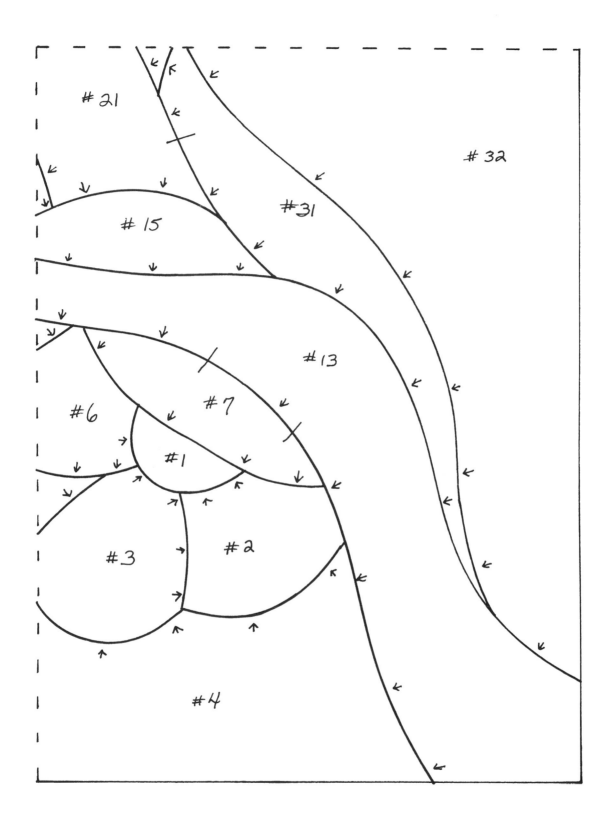

21

32

31

15

13

#6

7

#1

#3

2

#4

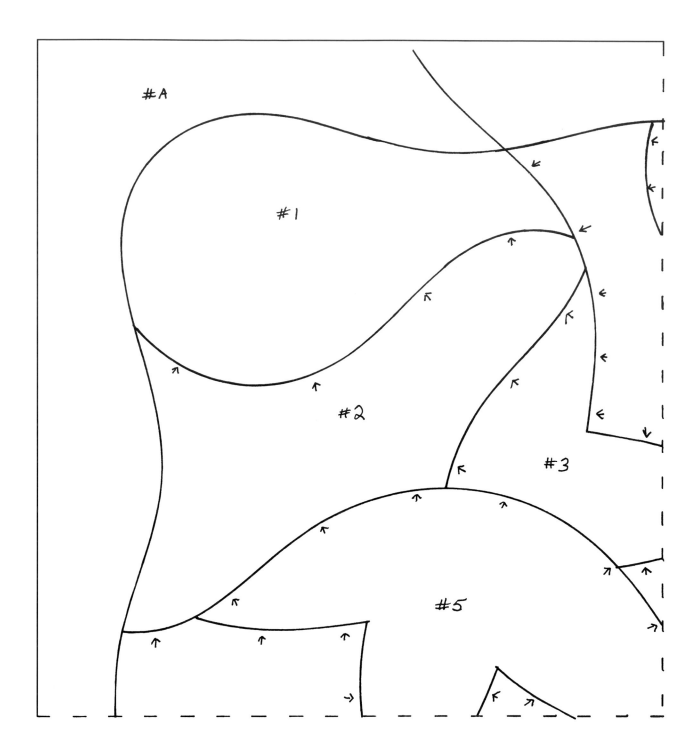

#A

#1

#2

#3

#5

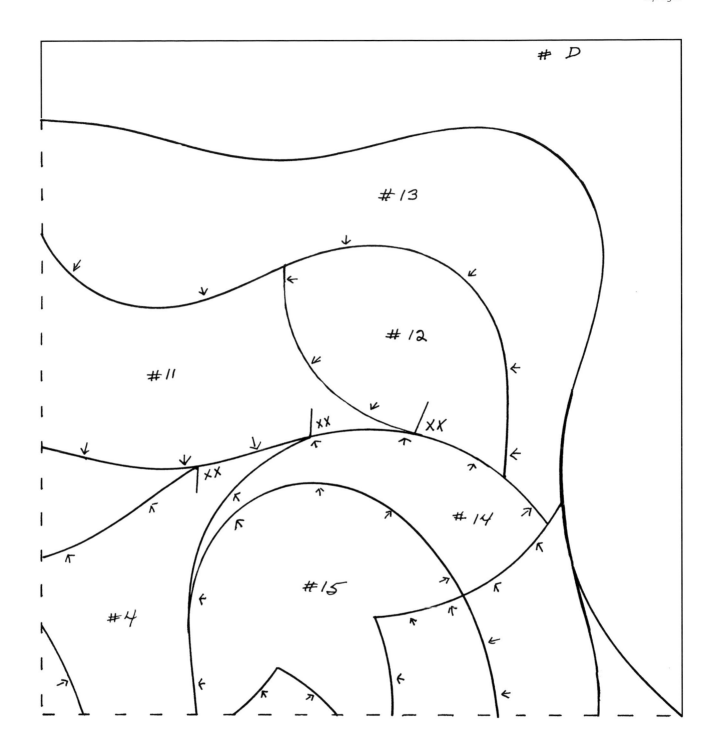

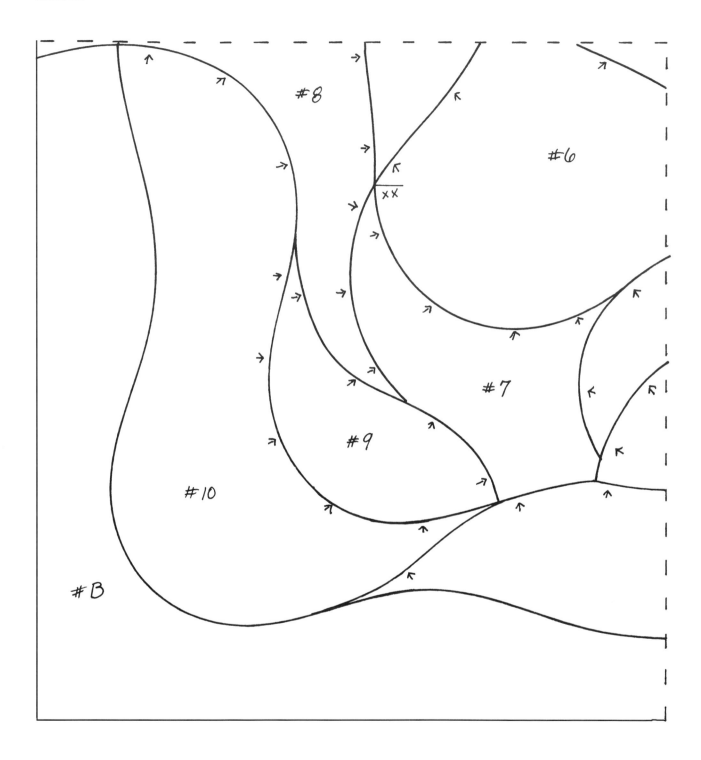

#8

#6

xx

#7

#9

#10

#B

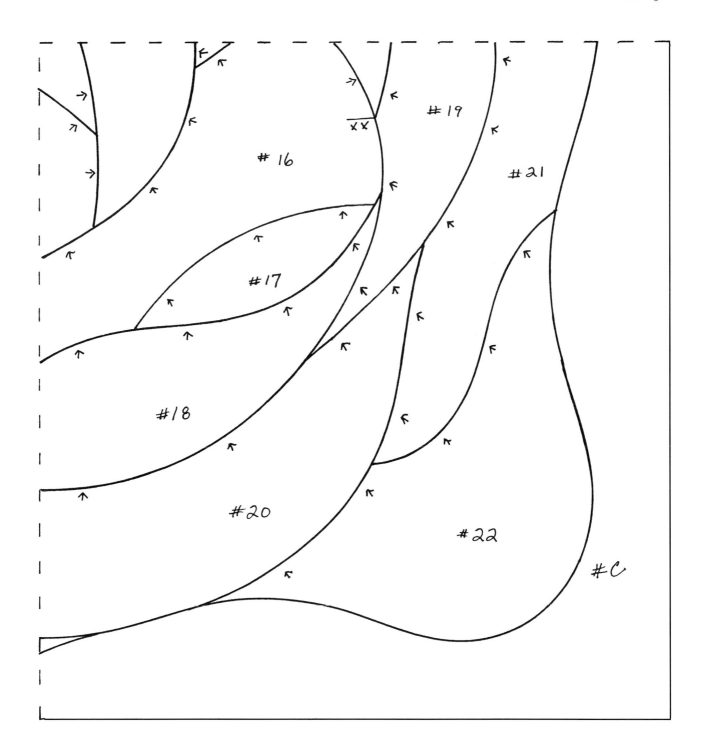

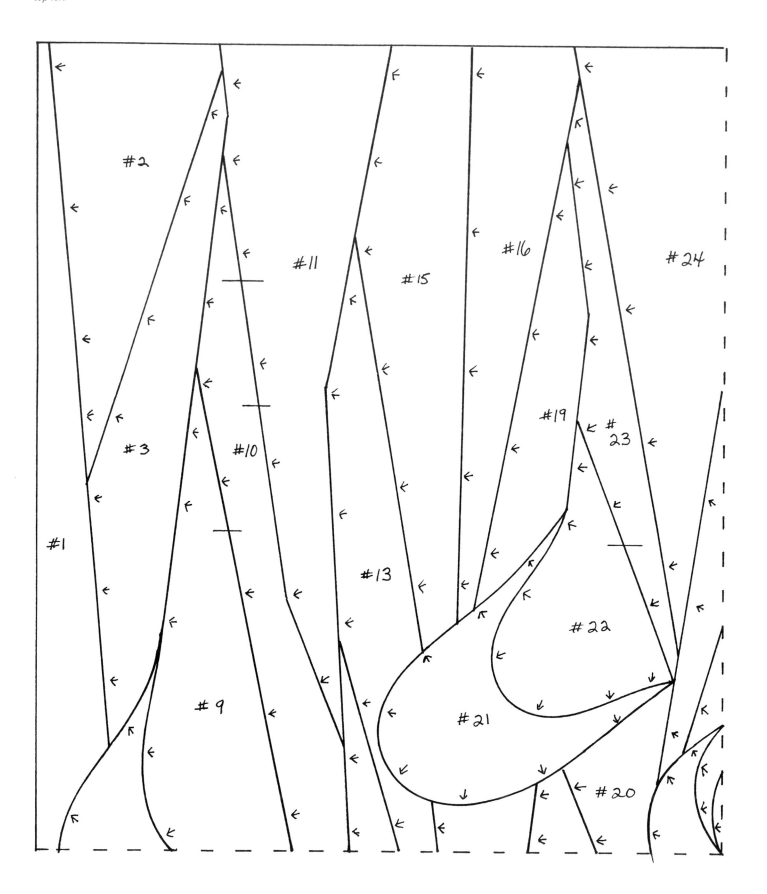

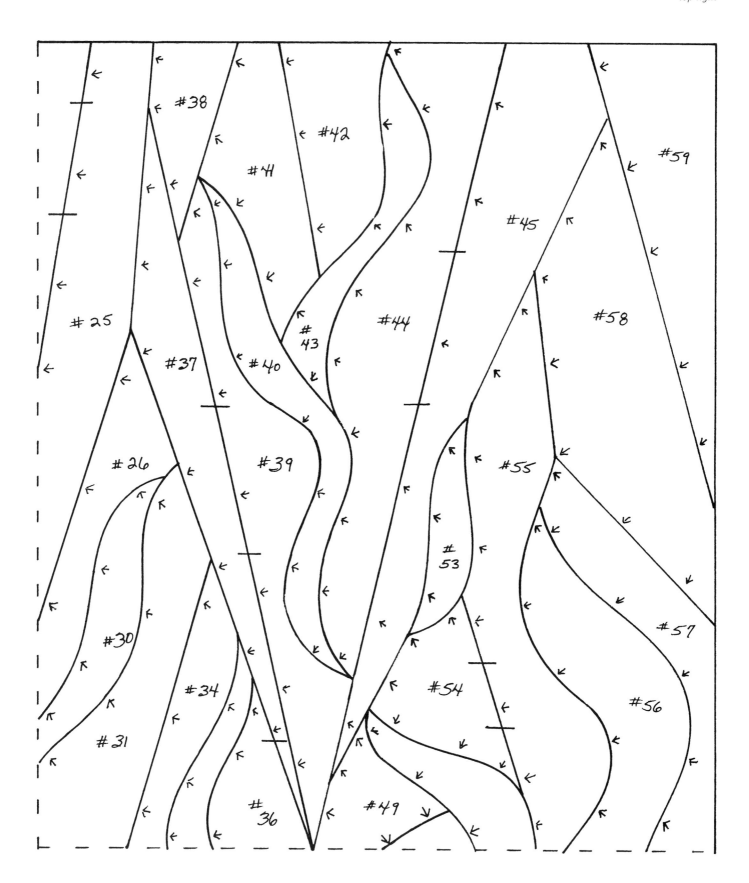

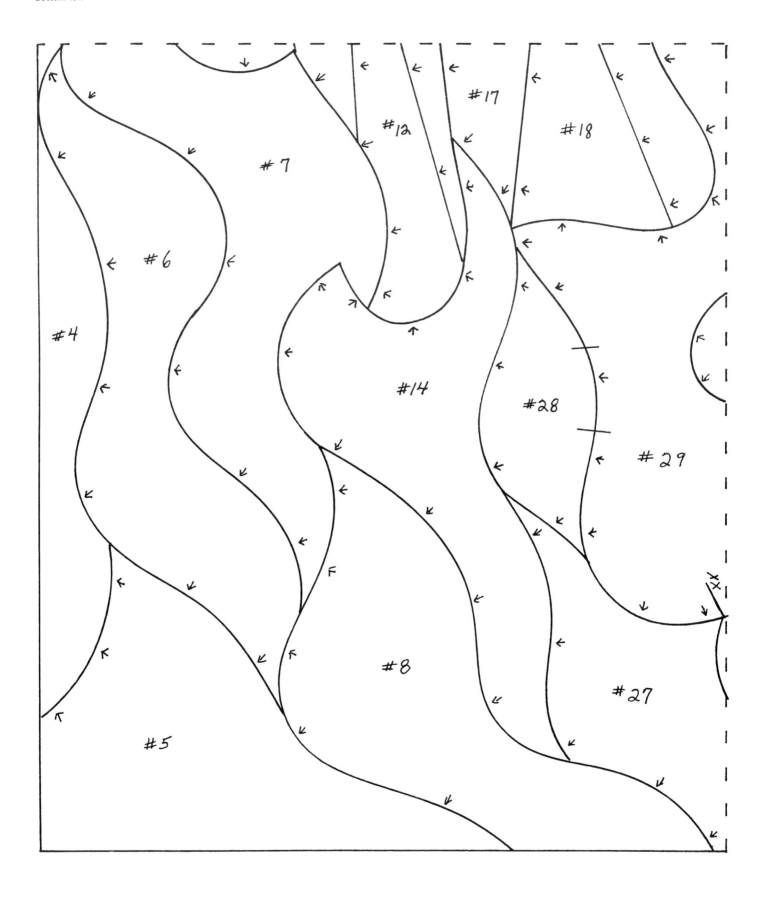

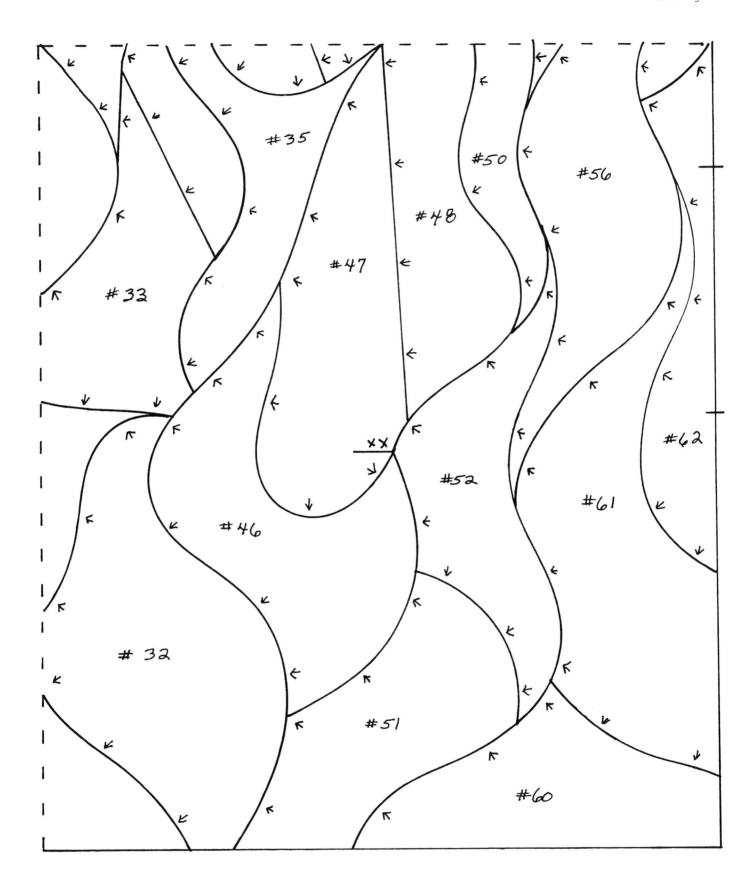

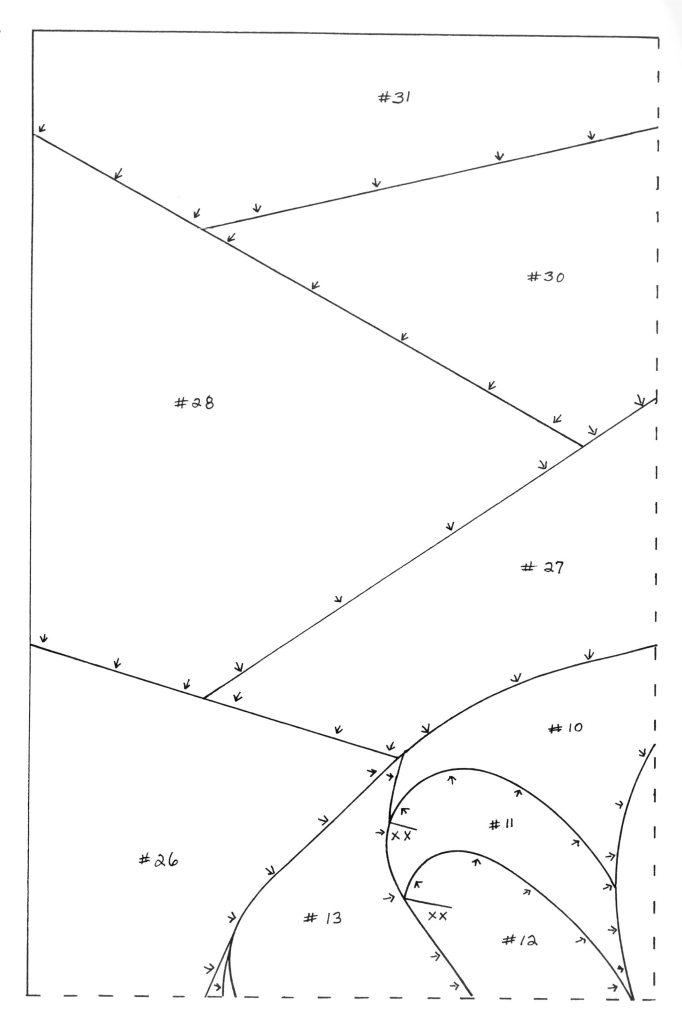

#31

#30

#28

#27

#10

#11

× ×

#26

#13

× ×

#12

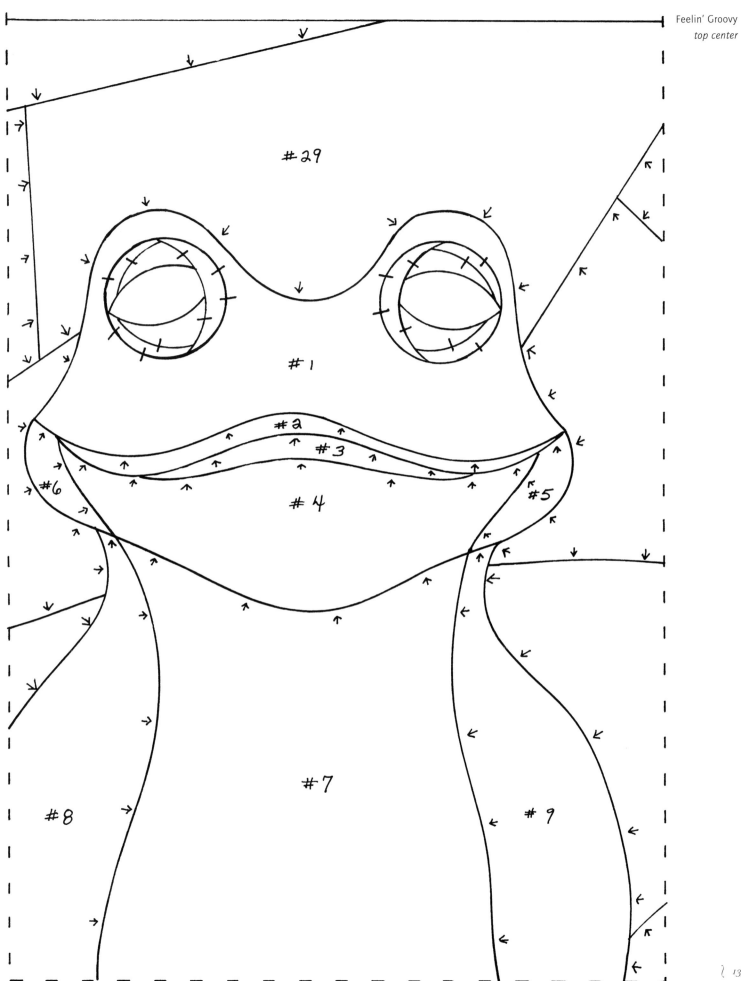

#29

#1

#2

#3

#6

#4

#5

#7

#8

#9

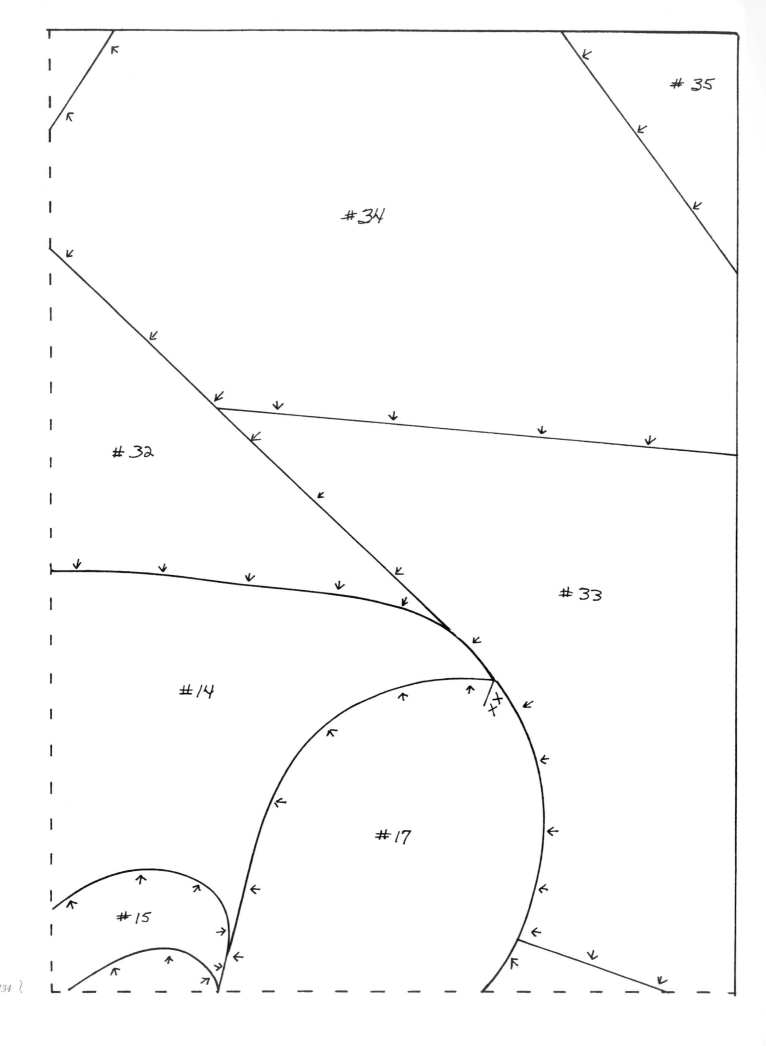

35

34

32

33

14

X
X

17

15

134

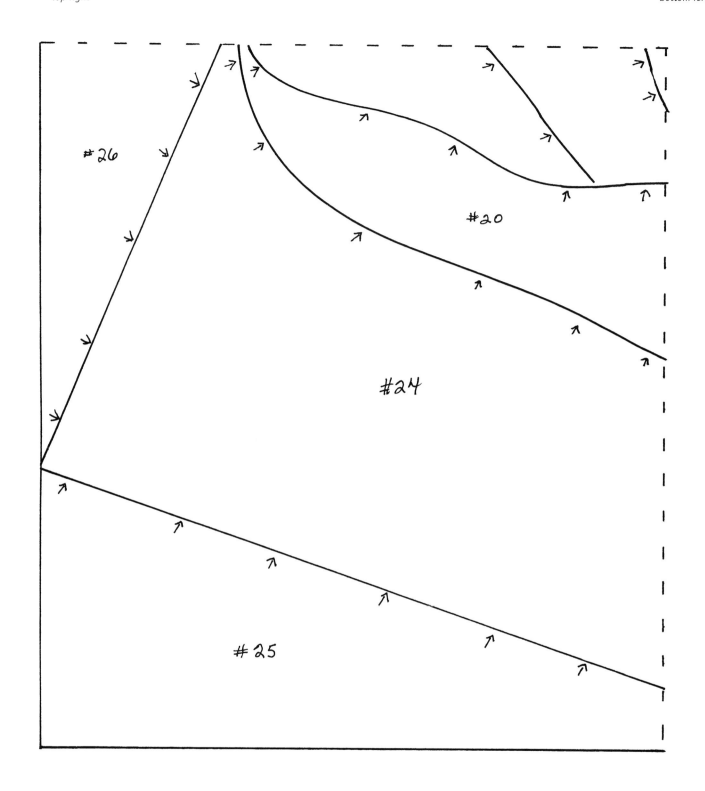

#26

#20

#24

#25

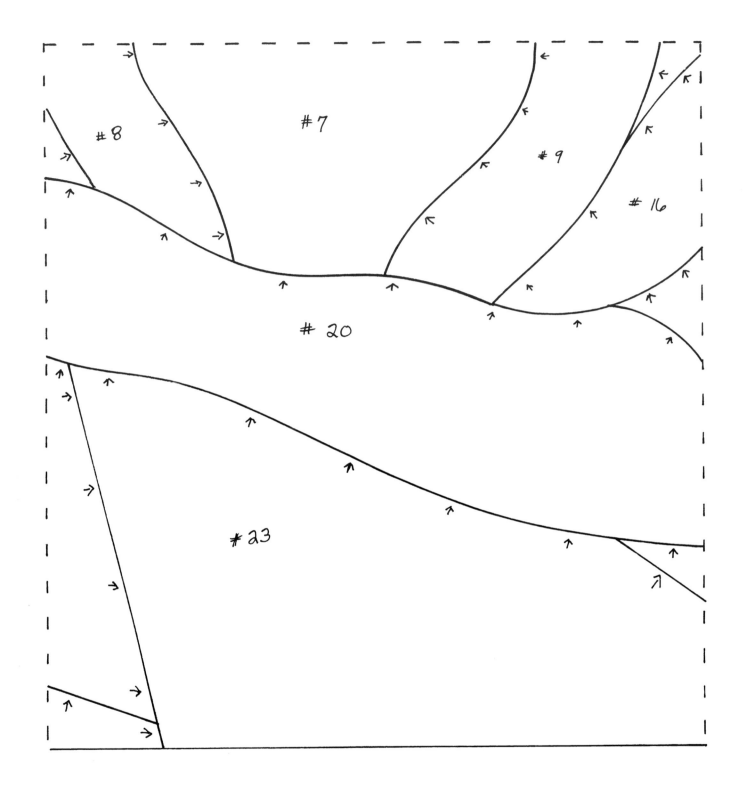

#8

#7

#9

#16

#20

#23

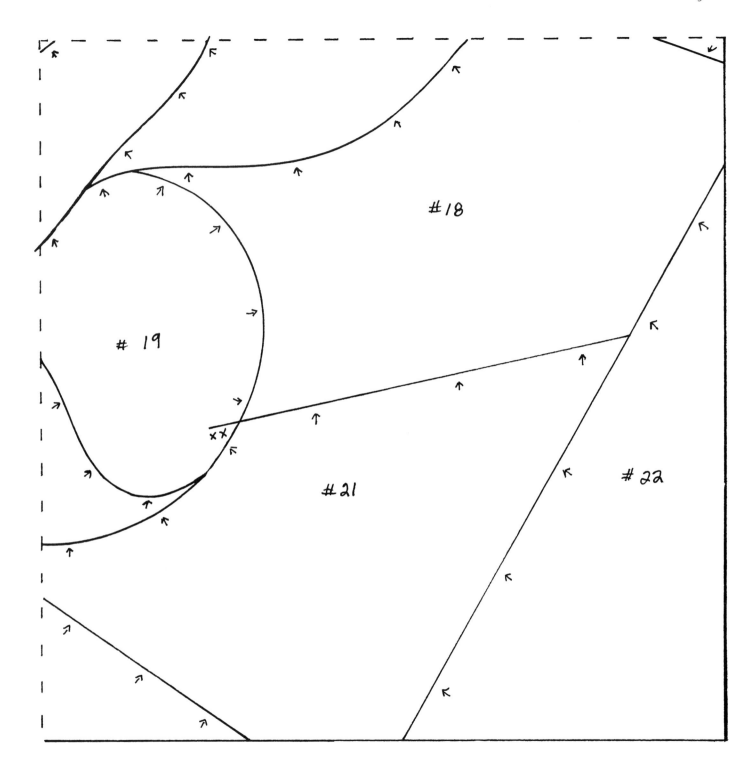

#18

19

#21

#22

Spiral Daisy
bottom right and
top left (upside down)

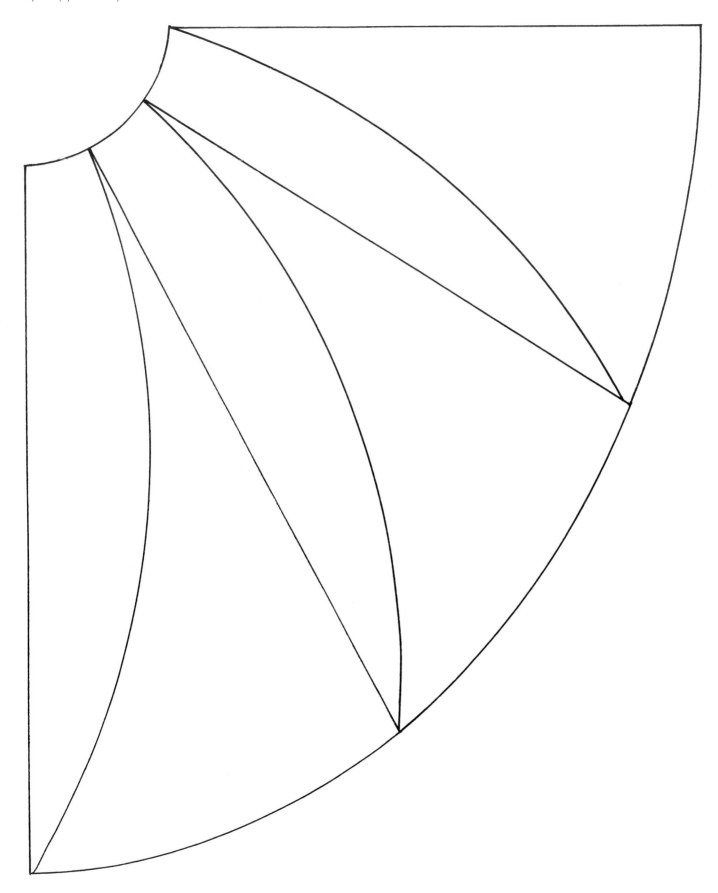

Spiral Daisy
*bottom left and
top right (upside down)*

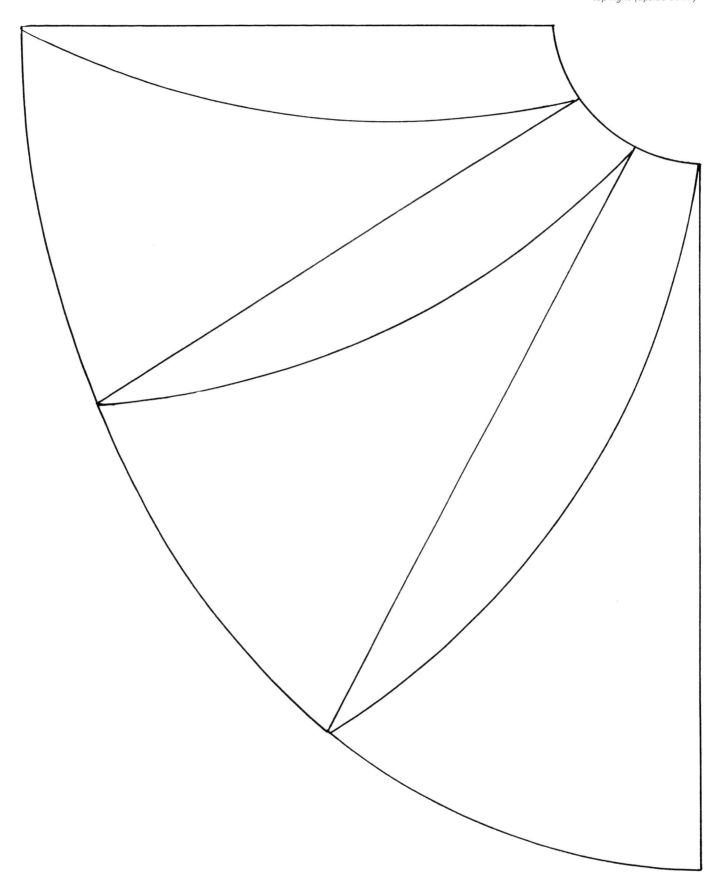

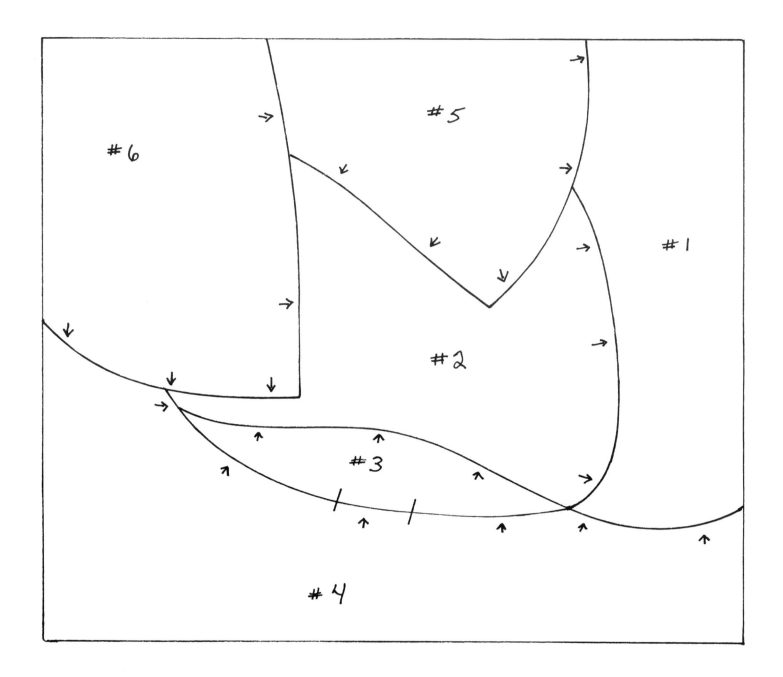

#6

#5

#1

#2

#3

#4

A Few Last Words

I feel strongly that the inspiration for my art, and the piecing technique I use to make it a reality, are special gifts given to me. I didn't realize how powerful these gifts could be until I started to use them!

As a woman and as a quilter I have dreams, hopes, and a few lofty goals I've set for myself. I achieved one of my goals by writing these book. Another is to use these gifts for both my personal fulfillment and the good of others. It's my hope that by sharing with you this technique and my work, I will encourage you to reach deep within yourself to bring forth the wonderful inspirations and visions that rest there, waiting for you to allow them to flow freely. My hope is that this book helps you to translate those great ideas to fabric and that you succeed in finding the potential of your gifts and share your work with others. For by sharing your enthusiasm, insights, and experiences you will enrich our world.

I would like to thank Denny, my wonderful husband and best friend, for his unwavering love and emotional support during my highs, lows, joys, and sorrows, not only while writing this book, but during our entire life together. And for his patience despite all the missed meals and oftentimes messy house!

I'd like to thank my sister, Augie Ellis, for her loving reassurance, advice, helpful critiques, and unlimited guidance.

I would like to express my gratitude to Susan Hart for her friendship, direction, and efforts in teaching me to sew better.

Also, I would like to acknowledge Desiree Vaughn and Joan and Bob Robinson for their help, generosity, and friendship.

My deepest appreciation to Anne Knudsen, executive editor at The Quilt Digest Press, for her editing skills, professional guidance, and patience. She made my dream a reality. Thank you, Anne! And many thanks to Sharon Hoogstraten, whose photographic expertise is unbelievable.

My appreciation also to Julia Anderson, Kim Bartko, and all those working behind the scenes to make this book special.

Special thanks to all my friends and students for their kind words, emotional support, and encouragement. I am truly grateful to you.